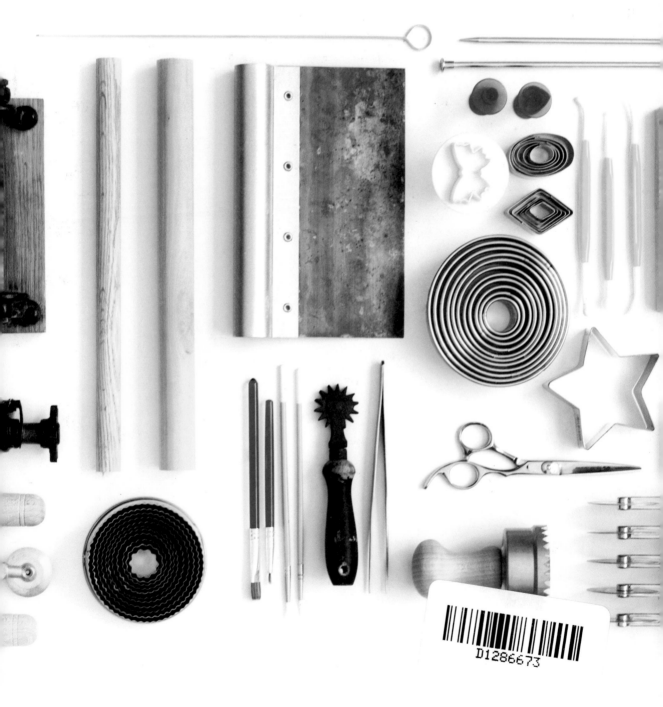

PASTA,
PRETTY PLEASE

PASTA,
PRETTY PLEASE

A VIBRANT APPROACH TO
HANDMADE NOODLES

LINDA MILLER NICHOLSON

PHOTOGRAPHS BY BRITTANY WRIGHT

WM
WILLIAM MORROW
An Imprint of HarperCollinsPublishers

HarperCollins books may be purchased for educational, business, or sales promotional use. For information, please email the Special Markets Department at SPsales@harpercollins.com.

FIRST EDITION

DESIGNED BY RENATA DE OLIVEIRA

PHOTOGRAPHS BY BRITTANY WRIGHT

Library of Congress Cataloging-in-Publication Data has been applied for.

ISBN 978-0-06-267493-7

18 19 20 21 22   LSC   10 9 8 7 6 5 4 3 2 1

FOR JONAS,
WHO ALWAYS SAID I COULD,

BENTLEY,
WHO ALWAYS QUESTIONS,

AND MOM,
WHO ALWAYS LOVES

CONTENTS

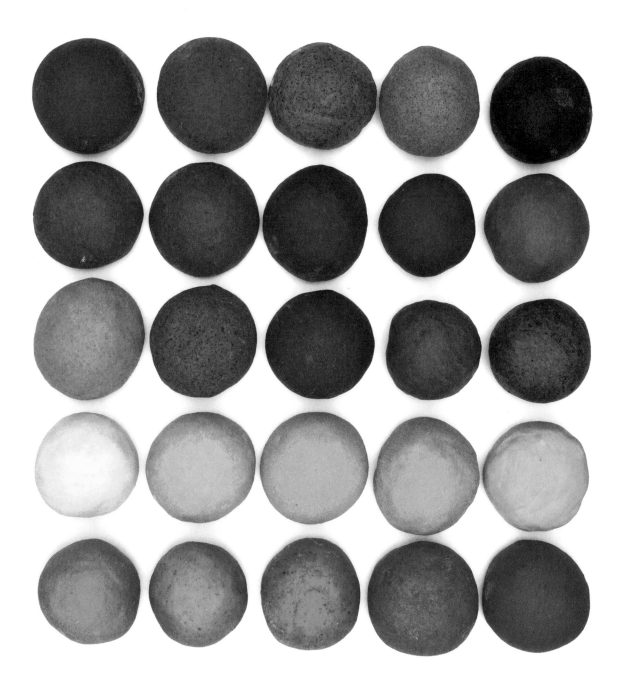

Guess what makes each color, and then turn to page 38 for the answers.

INTRODUCTION
WHY DO YOU DO THAT PASTA VOODOO THAT YOU DO?

Color, vitality, whimsy, and technique—think of this book as a treasured skeleton key that unlocks a joy-drenched world of prismatic pasta.

Many people see pretty pasta in pleasing, patterned colors and wonder why such a thing exists, only to be destroyed in one fell bite. Well, never mind health for a moment, let's talk philosophy. Soon, my precious, you will hear the story of how this Technicolor dreamcoat was woven, but the why is important too, and for that explanation we must turn toward Tibetan Buddhism, and with it, the concept of the sand mandala. You probably have a notion of what it is: a colorful, centric piece of art crafted out of dyed sand.

Sand mandalas signify the journey from ignorance to enlightenment. The designs are considered sacred to make, and long-trained monks who undertake a mandala possess willpower, patience, and perseverance. Monks creating sand mandalas must not only understand the significance in Buddhism, but also the internal personification, which is often the more difficult task. Mandalas instill lessons in both the monks and those lucky enough to witness the art, but after the ceremonies are completed and the public viewing is over, mandalas are swept into the nearest body of water. On the one hand, rivers, lakes, and seas will disperse the mandalas' symbolism far and wide, but more important, destroying a piece of art that was so painstakingly produced teaches us not to become attached to material objects.

Art cannot be possessed; it is something that should be enjoyed and embodied. Food, at the confluence of science and taste, amounts to edible art. When we are privileged, we know that we can create it again, taste it again, and hold it within the part of ourselves that is one of the most inexplicably important. It is a privilege worth acknowledging and sharing with those who may not have the same means, for food is the greatest equalizer, and commonality is something that the world needs much, much more of.

HOW I CAME TO THE WORLD OF PASTA

Hello, my name is Linda, and I'm a pastaholic. You are too, you say? Then you're in the right place. But let's back up and get to know each other a little bit, shall we? I mean, if you're going to take me in the kitchen, at least buy me a drink first.

I made my first batch of noodles when I was thigh-high to my grandmother, and she topped out at four foot eleven so I was a wee thing of about four. My parents didn't cook—they were very busy raising kids and starting a medical practice in Nowheresville, Idaho, having moved there when I was three and my half siblings were in the awkward throes of junior high. My father met my mother and her two children, a boy and a girl, in Southern California in the mid-seventies, and they wed a few years later. My mom is black, and so was her first husband, but my dad is as white as a Céline Dion song, so when I came out towheaded and screaming off-key, it was no big surprise.

For some reason, my parents thought it was a good idea to move away from our urban, progressive Los Angeles suburb and set up my father's family practice in a postage-stamp town in southern Idaho. While they were occupied with trying to make sure the town didn't lynch half our family (it wasn't that bad, but I do remember a lady accusing my mom of stealing me once in a department store), I was content hanging with my best friend, Slobber. He was a calf. My dad killed him one autumn with no warning, served me a hamburger made from his flesh, and catapulted me into a twenty-year stint as a vegetarian, but that's a tale for another tome.

Every summer they would ship me back to California to spend three months with my paternal grandparents, and during those three months I got lessons in cribbage, *Days of Our Lives*, and cooking, in that order. My grandpa was first-generation German, and his favorite dish to prepare was a chicken and noodle situation he had learned from his own grandfather. Gotta love the patrilineal passing of the cook's toque.

Either I demonstrated real skill, or I was just the lowest kid on the totem pole trifecta that consisted of Grandpa, Grandma, and me. However it happened, I got put on noodle duty every time. That may sound fun, but as a wisp of a girl with twigs for muscles operating a rolling pin on a wobbly table, I can assure you, it was not. At first, anyway. But something clicked, and every summer I got better at noodle making by hand. I would roll the dough into sheets, fold it onto itself, roll it again, and then sling it over the backs of chairs to let gravity take a turn. While the noodle sheets rested and I psyched myself up for another round behind the rolling pin, Grandma let me take sips off

the foamy top of her Michelob beer. For the first time in my young life, I felt like I was part of something.

A few years later, dying for a way to escape the vanilla subculture that existed in Idaho at the time, I discovered global cookbooks. I was drawn to any Italian cookbook I could find. The first was a ridiculously *bom chicka wah-wah* seventies number called *Romantic Italian Cooking: Authentic Recipes Just for Two*.

It was fortuitous because by that time (I was eleven), my parents were divorced and my siblings were grown, so my confused mom experienced my culinary triumphs and failures in the most amorous way possible. After Mom

and I had gazed longingly into each other's eyes over heart-shaped pizza for two, I sensed it was time to move on to more scholarly titles. Because I didn't eat meat at the time, pasta was a natural food to make and obsess over. I gleaned everything I could from mostly eighties-era cookbooks, such as *Giuliano Bugialli's Classic Techniques of Italian Cooking*.

By my mid-teens, I had a working theoretical and practical knowledge of Italian food—pasta especially—but none of it prepared me for a solo pilgrimage to Italy at age nineteen. Clad in patchwork leather shorts I stitched myself and armed with the street smarts of a kitten,

I careened alone across the motherland like a tornado, inhaling everything I could (food and otherwise, legal and otherwise) with the haphazard velocity only a teenage girl on a tear is capable of.

During that journey, I did all you'd expect of a free-spirited wild child—for I had not yet measured out my life with coffee spoons. I remember sneaking into the Colosseum at 2 a.m. so I could hurtle around the labyrinthine arena floor with my crazy new Roman friends.

We drank Strega until dawn and they taught me how to introduce myself properly in Italian, in contrast with "I love you, I'm clean," which is what I had been opening with for the previous few weeks after evidently mixing some bad intel with even worse linguistic comprehension. At least it explained all the gobsmacked looks I'd been getting. On the more innocent side, I also ate at least three gelati a day, alternating among my lifelong ride-or-die flavors, *nocciola*, *gianduja*, and *pistacchio*.

That trip was not fueled by money as much as by dreams and odd jobs along the way—did you know you could pay for a night's stay in a hostel by helping to cook (if you're lucky) and clean (if you must)? Early on, I spent what few extra lire (I'm dating myself) I had on restaurants in less expensive, more southerly cities like Brindisi and Napoli, but Capri nearly bankrupted me, and by the time I got to Roma, I was subsisting on crusty *pane* and gelato, trying to stretch what I had left.

Hunger and curiosity made me say yes to a pasta lunch prepared by the nonna of one of my new Italian friends, and I'm fortunate I did, because it was the best meal of the trip. She wanted to make me *spaghetti alla gricia*, which has guanciale in it, but I was vegetarian at the time. I brokenly pantomimed this to her, much to her disappointment. She did not see how guanciale—cured pork jowl—constituted meat, since it wasn't beef, and it was cut into such tiny pieces. I nodded assent and smiled bravely, mentally preparing myself to eat around chunks of pig cheek (current me thinks former me was an idiot, for guanciale is meltingly good), because I was graciously invited into someone's home, after all.

I think she must have seen the trepidation on my very non-poker face, because instead, she made us big, sloppy bowls of *cacio e pepe*, which I can close my eyes and taste to this day. People say the New York water is what sets New York bagels above any competition. Well, there is something about pecorino cheese from Lazio that makes your eyes roll back in your head and your mouth hang open like a star-struck sheep. Whipped with a frenzy of black pepper and whorls of spaghetti, pecorino is at its most luminous. I dreamed of that meal during the last, lean weeks of my first Italian adventure, but I didn't attempt to re-create it for at least a decade, not wanting to soil the memory.

A few years later—punctuated by a trifling amount of growing up—Jonas, my boyfriend of three months who is now my husband, informed me that he was transferring to Italy for his job, and he had negotiated an open-ended ticket for me, should I wish to join him. His exact words were: "I like you enough to bring you with me, but not enough to stay here for you." Really, what person in their right mind would *not* move to Italy if the stars aligned? I was finishing a graduate degree I could easily do remotely, and despite having dated him for only a short time, I knew he wasn't a psychopath, so I went along. We lived in Torino, the heart of the Piedmont region and, in my very unbiased opinion, the ne plus ultra of *la vita bella*.

I steeped myself in Piemontese culture in those few years, but at first it was a land grab for knowledge that began with the pronunciation of *cucchiaio*. *Cucchiaio* is a four-syllable word that means "spoon" in Italian, and it's initially hard for an American to pronounce— even if that American had, very recently prior to said pronouncing, nabbed an undergrad degree in Latin.

Jonas and I had been there for a week and decided to quiz each other on basic words like *forchetta*, *cucchiaio*, and *coltello*. We were both really tripped up on *cucchiaio*, which sounds like "coo-key-aye-oh." Knowing we needed to commit it to memory, we decided to lob it back and forth across the table in a very quiet, very bright *ristorante*. If you've spent much time there, you know that the lights are almost always too bright in restaurants in Italy. As is the case when you've had plenty of wine and you're talking quickly to try to outdo your tablemate, our voices began to escalate. Suddenly we looked around and saw that we were on full display for being the two *pazzi stranieri* animatedly shout-singing, *"Spoon spoon spoon spoon spoon."* Suffice it to say I will never forget how to pronounce the Italian word for spoon!

Before Torino, I wondered how I could possibly eat pasta nearly every night of the week and not get sick of it. Little did I know. When I moved there, I viewed pasta as a finite thing, completely unaware just how vast the canon of shapes combined with sauces could be. I came to realize I could barely scratch the surface of pasta in my lifetime, let alone in a few short years.

Now that we have been back in Washington State for ten years, with barely annual Torino trips to appease us, the only way through has been constant daily pasta making. Then, when my son, Bentley Danger, turned five a few years ago, he went through one of *those* phases. Nothing on his plate could touch anything else. So help you if you tried to sneak any vegetable besides a carrot into him. I tried pureeing spinach into smoothies—nope. Tucking greens under the cheese in pizza—no way, with a side of dramatic gagging.

One day I realized I had made green pasta dough using nettles plenty of times. Vegetable-dyed pasta has a centuries-old history in Italy, so why wasn't I using other vegetables in my own noodles too?

I banked on Bentley not being able to taste the vegetable ingredients, and I confess to telling the parental white lie that all the colors were edible Play-Doh. That proved to be the ticket, and suddenly he was not only eating vegetables in every color of the rainbow, he was also in the kitchen with me, playing with the dough and providing me with a lifetime of treasured mama-son memories. He eats vegetables like a boss now, no matter the form, and I'm happy I found a way to get him over the tiny hurdle without giving up and resorting to chicken nuggets on the regular.

And my own obsession grew. Single-color strands gave way to two-sided noodles, and that quickly veered into rainbow territory. Then I realized that with a few basic tools and some imagination, I could make a whole mess of patterns right on my pasta sheets. These days it's not uncommon to find me sneaking a photo of the design on a stranger's shirt, stalking wallpaper like a wallflower, or ordering a pair of shoes just

so I can turn the pattern on their toe-box into pasta.

However unconventional it may be, I have found my art, and with that, my true path. My parents always cautioned me to go the practical route—find something dependable and, well, depend on it. In today's society, I'm not sure that is the best advice. It's undeniably important to develop a foundation and work hard and smart, but if I hadn't challenged the norms and put diamond dowels in round holes time and time again, I fear I would never have found the thing that satisfies my soul, not just my monthly creditors.

It will please me to the sweetest end if you want to make the noodles in my book, but I don't expect colored pasta to be the other side of your BFF heart necklace as it is mine. I do hope that in joining me for a part of this journey, no matter how young or old you are, how busy or free, you are inspired to set aside moments every day to pursue what you really want in life, even if you don't know exactly what that is. Dedicating the time to figure it out is enough that eventually a door will burst open like a Watermelon Bubblicious bubble, and you'll know, without a dust mote of doubt, it's right.

While I have many people to thank for my journey into the colorful, nutritious world of pasta art, I'm fulfilled to the brink of tears that I can attribute my current career and lifelong passion primarily to the most important little guy in my life, Bentley.

MY COOKING STYLE: THE PAST, THE PRESENT, AND THE FUTURE

Here's a little history lesson that will blow your mind if you're pasta-obsessed. Let's talk for a moment about tortelli, ravioli, and gnocchi. What we think of as ravioli—filled pasta—used to be known as tortelli, which is the word still commonly used throughout Italy. Ravioli, rather, were shaped dumplings rolled in such a way as to mimic the round-rooted turnip

called *rabiola* in Latin or *rape* nowadays. In other words, ravioli was a type of gnocchi—pasta dumplings—rolled into the shape of tiny turnips.

I find that anecdote, gleaned from *Giuliano Bugialli's Classic Techniques of Italian Cooking*, fascinating from an evolutionary perspective, because both language and our manipulation of culinary ingredients constantly metamorphose. I don't presume to comprehend the entirety of Italian pasta, because it is ever-changing, but those of us who endeavor to innovate should do so with as much awareness and respect for the traditional versions as possible.

Breaking that down further, I know I'll irk some Italian traditionalists with my—shall we say colorful?—approach to pasta, but that is certainly not my intention. I am constantly learning everything I can about noodles that exist or once existed somewhere in the world, but when I set out to make my daily batches of dough, the resulting pasta is mine alone. I began this section by showing that even something as pervasively known throughout the world as ravioli was at one point a completely different thing. By this I mean to gently nudge purists to see that things change, and most of the time it's okay. Sometimes it's even for the better.

After all, we wouldn't have burrata cheese without the enterprising minds of some innovative Pugliese cheesemakers

in the 1950s. Looking for a way to use up the scraps left over from mozzarella production, they began to make a final "kitchen sink" cheese at the end of the day. They kneaded the mozzarella scraps into a vessel-like form, poured in some fresh cream for binding, and tied it up in a pretty topknot. Thus, burrata was born, and the world—well, Puglia—rejoiced! Because burrata is so perishable, it rarely traveled outside that region until recently, when global demand caused cheesemakers to duplicate burrata (not quite as well, but still) with pasteurized dairy.

Which brings me to my next point. Those cheesemakers employed a very important Italian notion called . . .

CUCINA POVERA

Cucina povera literally means "poor kitchen," but there's more to the story. *Cucina povera* has roots in southern Italy, and hearkens back especially to several postwar periods when food was scarce for everyday people. Beyond just the notion that nothing should go to waste, enterprising cooks found ways to cobble together ingredients like flour, legumes, wild greens, and typically discarded parts of vegetables, such as turnip tops, so they could feed their families.

Meat was expensive and uncommon, and if it was procured, no part went unused. Famous dishes borne of *cucina povera* often contain organ meats like tripe, brains, and liver. Some families could afford to buy tripe only once a week, and it was sold preboiled for convenience from shops called *tripperie* that were as common as vegetable vendors in any given *villagio* at the turn of the twentieth century. Those who could not afford the tripe itself had to make do with the broth used to boil it. It was a welcome flavoring for cheap legumes and grains, such as chickpeas and rice.

Pasta is the very definition of *cucina povera*. By mixing water (or eggs) with flour, forming it into a paste, then somehow cutting and drying it, early noodle makers the world over were preserving flour to make it last over long periods of famine, *miseria*, or swashbuckling adventures.

Nowadays *cucina povera* has come to mean a celebration of simple, inexpensive ingredients coaxed together in inventive ways, so as to waste nothing. While this book has a few pricy ingredients (only because of their current popularity or trendiness), at its core it is just flour, eggs, and things that grow from the earth. Granted, they are woven together in a manner a Genovese villager in the fifteenth century might

consider sorcery or heresy or both, but it's all in the spirit of resourceful Italian innovation.

TOOLS OF THE TRADE

Pasta making need not be complex. If you have a rolling pin, a bench scraper, and some elbow grease, you can make noodles. I'm in the habit of using a wine bottle to roll out a batch of pasta when I'm in hotel rooms if I'm lucky enough to have a means to boil water, just to keep my skills sharp. Nevertheless, I've put together a list of some items that will make your life slightly easier if you're interested in scaling up your pasta station. (See also page 69, "The Means to Roll and Sheet Pasta Dough.")

SHEET PANS

I like to use half sheet pans with lids, sometimes called baker's half sheets or jellyroll pans, to store all my fresh pasta until I bake it. The pans are usually aluminum, and the thickness doesn't matter a whole lot (unless you're using them for something else), but if you're investing in a few new ones, I suggest buying them in a set that includes the plastic lids, as I have noticed that not every lid fits every pan across all manufacturers. The lids snap on to the top of the pans and are raised above the pans about an inch, which is convenient for storing unruly pasta that lies higher

than the edges of the pan. A standard half pan is 13 by 18 inches, more or less, and it is the right size for a sheet of parchment folded in half crosswise.

Half sheet pans are manageable to carry and fit inside most refrigerators, but if you have a smaller fridge, you may consider scaling down to quarter pans. Conversely, if you're strong as an ox, plan to make industrial quantities of pasta, and have all the room in the world, a full sheet pan may be the way to go.

PARCHMENT PAPER

I use a lot of parchment paper in pasta making. It's great for lining pans so that pasta doesn't stick to them and also makes a very nice sling from which to slide pasta directly into the boiling water, eliminating the need to hand-mangle sometimes delicate pieces of pasta such as gnocchi, gnudi, or even ravioli if you've forgotten to flour the bottom and the filling is especially wet. Even if pasta is stuck to the parchment, once it all hits the boiling water it will dislodge, whereas if you try to pry wet pasta off parchment with your hands or a spatula, the pasta will often tear.

Parchment gets pricy when you buy tiny rolls from the grocery store, but if you have the space, it's very inexpensive in bulk. Both half-and full-size sheets of parchment are available in packets of 1,000 and cost less than a nickel a sheet when you buy 1,000. If you can find only the more common full sheets, fold them in half to fit inside a half sheet pan.

PLASTIC WRAP

If you go as mad for pasta as I have, you are going to use a *lot* of plastic wrap to store your dough. May I advise you again to buy in bulk? I prefer the 18-inch width, as it makes covering everything easier, but go with what works in your space. Unless you already have a cutter setup, be sure to purchase a box with the means to cut. A convenient search term to locate this plastic wrap is "PVC foodservice wrap film with slide cutter."

STOCKPOT

I recommend *at least* a 6-quart pot. I am in the habit of boiling my pasta in a large stockpot, regardless of how small the batch is. It's partly because I'm lazy and I know just how much salt and water to put into my trusty old pot, but also because it's *always* better to use more water, not less, when boiling pasta. When you add a lot of pasta to a little boiling water, it will take a long time for that water to come back to boil. Conversely, when you add pasta to plenty of boiling water, it will barely stop the boil. Temperature consistency is important for cooking al dente fresh pasta, as if it heats back up too slowly, it will make the noodles both mushy and tough at the same time. Ain't nobody got time for that. A single batch

of dough in this book is designed to boil in 4 quarts water, if this at all sways your pot purchasing preferences.

STACKABLE FOOD DRYING TRAYS WITH NETS

Stackable pasta drying trays have mesh material inside a wooden frame. The pasta rests directly on the net so air can flow all around it. The trays are rectangular and come with removable dowels so that you can stack many trays on top of one another on a relatively small countertop footprint. This stackability comes in handy when you're making a large quantity in a small space. They can also be used to dry foods

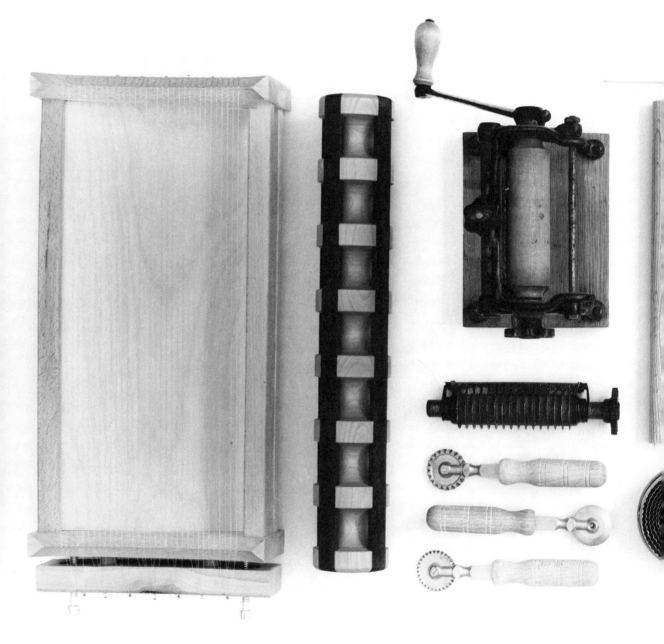

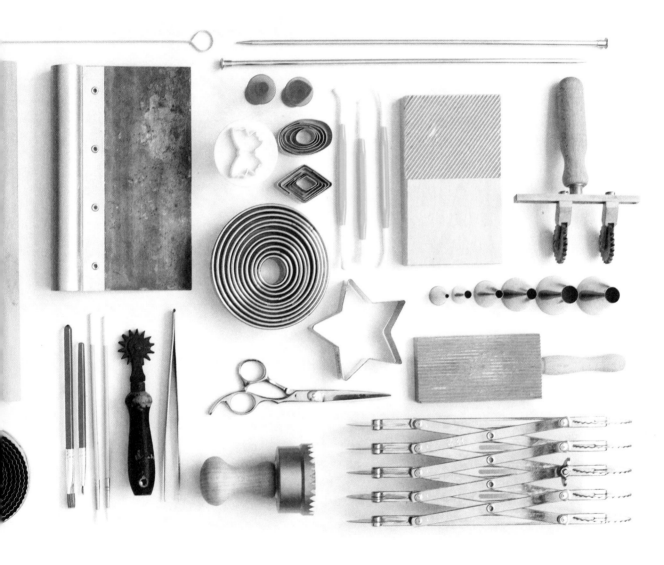

such as fruits, vegetables, herbs, and mushrooms. Look for the manufacturer Eppicotispai, available online.

DRYING RODS, RACKS, OR DOWELS

The best, cheapest, and easiest way you can hang long pasta to dry at home is to go to your local hardware store and purchase some dowels. You can drape long noodles over them and use them to hold tubular noodles such as cannelloni in a circular form until they're dry enough to hold their shape. I recommend dowels with about a ¾-inch diameter, but if you already have ½- or 1-inch dowels lying around and you don't want to make a

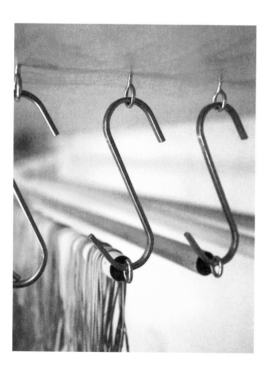

special trip, they'll do just fine. I keep mine 48 inches long, the length they come at the hardware store. If you don't have a good place to keep rods that long, saw them shorter yourself or have the hardware store do it for you—it's usually a free service.

You can make your dowel system basic or complex. Resting the dowels between two chairbacks works well, and chances are you already have the chairs. If you want to get fancy, you can rig up your own dowel rack with S hooks suspended from screw-eyes beneath your upper kitchen cabinets. It's a low-profile, easily removable way to get drying space on the cheap. Multiple S hooks linked together allow you to raise and lower the dowels for easier placement of noodles.

BENCH SCRAPER

A bench scraper, sometimes called a pastry scraper or pastry cutter, is essential for handling pasta. Used for everything from prying sticky pasta sheets up off the bench to cleaning the work surface after a session, this tool is indispensable. Size matters here, friends. Look for one with an edge that is between 6 and 9 inches for maximum ease of use.

ROLLING CUTTER

Many of you will already have a rolling cutter in your kitchen arsenal from pie

making. It has a rolling wheel at the bottom that is either straight or fluted, and a handle extends upward from the wheel. The very best rolling cutters have wheels made of brass and last a long time. An online search for "rolling pasta cutter" or "brass pasta wheel" will yield plenty of results. I recommend both a fluted (sometimes called "festooned") and a straight rolling cutter, for making straight or jagged finishing cuts along the edges of your pasta. Note that fluted rolling cutters come in various sizes. The "teeth" at the end of the wheel are wider or narrower, which determines the width of the zipper pattern on the pasta sheet.

SILICONE SUSHI MAT/GNOCCHI BOARD

In pasta making as in life, some of the smallest moments can be the most transformative. Take, for instance, the first time I rolled a sheet of pliant pasta against a silicone sushi mat and I realized I could stop harassing my husband into building me the biggest gnocchi board known to man so that I could make grooved, tubular pasta all day and all night and every second in between.

The silicone sushi mat solves so many problems because it's lightweight, has grip and texture to impart grooves,

and is bigger than most gnocchi boards, enabling you to make cool shapes such as paccheri and cannelloni, not to mention smaller grooved shapes like gnocchi, cavatelli, and garganelli. In short, get one. You'll find them at most Asian grocers, on Amazon, and elsewhere online. Lékué makes a good one. They're inexpensive and worth their weight in pasta-maker gold.

If old school is your thing and you opt for a gnocchi board rather than a silicone sushi mat, I recommend buying one as large as you can find, or making one yourself if you're handy with a table saw.

STAINLESS-STEEL ROUND CUTTER SET

Round cutters (sometimes called cookie cutters) are very handy for cutting shapes, making emoji ravioli, and cutting out pasta in general. I use both fluted and plain-edged, but I would start with plain-edged if I could choose only one.

PLUNGER CUTTERS

Typically sold in cake-decorating shops for fondant art, these babies will save your fingers when making big patterns across pasta sheets. Note that they are less expensive if you purchase them in a set, and plenty are available online.

Having the variety of a set gives you more creative freedom to make whatever patterns you desire rather than having to go out and hunt down new cutters every time a holiday or occasion rolls around.

FOOD-SAFE PAINTBRUSHES

A selection of small, soft-bristled food-safe paintbrushes in various sizes is very handy for moistening pasta, as when you're adhering two sheets together.

WATER SPRAY BOTTLE

I like to use a clean water spray bottle with a very fine mist setting to dampen pasta sheets as they dry out during pasta making.

RAVIOLI PIN

A ravioli pin is a rolling pin designed with special recessed holes in it that define uniform pieces of ravioli when rolled over a filled pasta sheet. None of the recipes in this book require you to have one, because it's such a specialized tool, but it's a very convenient way to quickly make a large number of consistently sized ravioli. Repast Supply Co. makes beautiful ravioli pins in both wood and stainless steel.

PASTA BIKE

A pasta bike is an adjustable rolling cutter with several wheels that each cut a line across a sheet of pasta. It is good for cutting large sheets into smaller shapes

where uniformity is key—cutting out many tiny squares for garganelli, for example. A single rolling cutter can accomplish the same task in a bit more time, and honestly, I rarely break out my pasta bike, preferring the precision of personally making every cut over the economy of scale. Nevertheless, it's a fun toy, and again, it comes in both flute-edged and straight versions.

REPURPOSING

Sometimes my ideas are bigger than my arsenal of kitchen tools. When that happens, I am never afraid to repurpose and grab something like a cheese grater to make texture on gnocchi, or use a broomstick to hang fettuccine to dry. Don't feel as if you must go out and buy a bunch of fancy new kitchen equipment to tackle pasta. After all, people have been making it for centuries with little more than flour, water, and their hands. Look around your kitchen and see if there are things you already own that can serve more than one purpose.

THE SECRET TO COLORED PASTA: VEGETABLES, HERBS, AND SUPERFOODS (PLUS SOME OTHER KEY INGREDIENTS)

While I began my colored pasta journey as a way to get nutrient-dense foods into my son, Bentley, I must admit that I'm equally excited about creating a rainbow using pronounceable ingredients, not factory-invented colors. This section isn't meant to make health claims, but I want to give you some background on the foods I use to make pasta dough, and maybe a tidbit or two on why I—and some fancy clinically qualified people—think they're worth consuming.

AÇAI BERRIES
The açai berry looks like a small grape and comes from the açai palm, which is indigenous to Brazil, Trinidad, and northern South America. It has a mild berry taste with faint undertones of chocolate. I use it in freeze-dried, powdered form for pasta making. Açai is considered a low-sugar antioxidant powerhouse. It's available online and in most health food stores and better supermarkets.

ACTIVATED CHARCOAL
Activated charcoal is used medically to treat overdose and poisoning, because drugs and toxins can bind to it. We use a negligible concentration in pasta; I wouldn't advise feeding your Romeo black noodles if you happen upon him poisoned, as it will have no effect. It's also used as a teeth-whitener, but it's so messy that I haven't gotten around to trying it in my very white bathroom.

Activated charcoal is different from the charcoal ash you get from burning wood, so please don't use that. Always purchase food-grade activated charcoal, and I prefer that made from bamboo over other woods, because it is finer and mixes easily into pasta dough.

You can also use squid ink to make black pasta dough, but it has a fishy taste, and since the recipes in this book mix many colors together, I elected to go with neutral-flavored activated charcoal to achieve black.

AVOCADOS
There's probably not much I can say about them that you don't already know,

but my favorite fact is that avocados are also known as alligator pears. That's the kind of tidbit that feeds my inner geek for days. As far as the health stuff is concerned, avocados are the only fruit that provide a substantial amount of monounsaturated fatty acids, and they contain nearly twenty vitamins and minerals.

RED BEETS
I love beets. You might not feel the same way. Regardless, please make at least one of the beet-containing doughs in this book. I promise you'll hardly taste them, and it's a mission of mine to convert haters to lovers through covert sorcery, a.k.a. finding just the right beet ratio to make them sing. Also, canned beets are the devil, and if you've only ever had them that way, give them a fresh shot. Beets really can't be beat, as they are a rich source of folate and manganese and also contain thiamine, riboflavin, vitamin B$_6$, and magnesium.

Note that color can be a bit inconsistent among red beets, so if color is your main motivating factor, you can obtain the most vibrant results by using frozen beets, in which much of the water is evaporated.

BLUEBERRIES
It took me awhile to come around to fruit as a color and flavor ingredient in pasta dough, but blueberries are what finally lured me, with their pure purple pigment and not overly sweet taste. Bonus points for being antioxidant rich.

BUCKWHEAT
Buck, you ain't no wheat at all, you're just an impasta! Buckwheat is actually a seed, not a grass like wheat, and it's most closely related to sorrel, knotweed, and rhubarb. I like buckwheat because it's high in protein, promotes good digestion, and grows easily, so it doesn't usually require a lot of pesticides or chemicals.

BURRATA
Burrata is a superfood in the sense that it's super damn pleasurable to put in your mouth. In case you've been living under a cheese-free rock, burrata looks like mozzarella on the outside, but inside there's a layer of *stracciatella*—shreds of cheese curd mixed with cream—that sets it apart from any and all cheese competitors. Put it this way: If a ball of burrata was rolling down a mountain toward you, your best option would be to lie flat and open wide. Of course we could say something about the calcium in the dairy that composes it, but burrata needs no justification for existence, because it's the most magnificent food to emerge from the twentieth century.

BUTTERFLY PEA FLOWERS
I'm sorry to be the one to pop your cherry on this, but butterfly pea flowers,

native to tropical equatorial Asia, are handily called *Clitoria ternatea* in Latin. That's because the flowers have the shape of human female genitals. So I don't know if it's lucky or unlucky that when you order them online (Amazon is your best bet), they arrive dried.

In any case, they are fun to play with. Steep them in hot water and drop in lemon to color the water more pinkish purple, or baking soda to turn it deeper blue.

Ayurvedic medicine claims that butterfly pea flowers enhance memory and are antidepressant and anti-stress. They're also antioxidant rich, and let's face it, anything that's blue and naturally occurring absolutely must be made into pasta.

CACAO POWDER

Cacao powder is made from raw, unroasted cocoa beans that are cold-pressed to remove the fat and retain the helpful enzymes. Cacao is mood-boosting and antioxidant rich and provides minerals like magnesium, iron, potassium, and calcium.

In pasta making, I do not recommend that you ever substitute cocoa for cacao. The resulting noodles will be sweet and cloying as opposed to nuanced and rich.

CARROTS

Old-school carrots—we're talking pre-1600s here—were white, purple, and yellow. It wasn't until the seventeenth century that the enterprising Dutch, momentarily bored of dike building, developed a new strain of carrot that contained higher amounts of beta-carotene. It was orange. This fashionable new carrot was all the rage because it was a celebration of William of Orange, a dude who led the Dutch in revolt against the Spanish in the late 1500s that eventually begat the independence of the Dutch Republic. This is a significant condensation of a broader (and true!) tale that you should look up if you ever get as bored as the Dutch clearly were of dike building.

At the end of the day we're left with beta-carotene, which really is quite good for you as a source of vitamins A, C, K, and B_8, folate, potassium, iron, copper, and magnesium.

CHESTNUTS

Chestnuts are a low-fat nut, but they're high in fiber and folate. They're the only nut to contain vitamin C, though not in significant measure. Chestnuts and Italy go way, way back. The largest and oldest known chestnut tree in the world is called Hundred Horse Chestnut and is located on the eastern slope of Mount Etna in Sicily. It's estimated to be between two thousand and four thousand years old. Italians use chestnuts to make pasta, cake, and even beer.

EGGS

Eggs are nature's most perfect food, not to be confused with burrata (see page 21) which is man's most perfect food creation. Do I really need to tell you why they're good for you?

All the egg-based doughs in this book were initially developed using organic eggs from my flock of chickens and ducks. I regularly weigh their eggs, and they come out to anywhere from 1.6 to 2.1 ounces. By egg grading standards, the vast majority of them would be considered medium-size, at about 1.7 ounces. Therefore, I altered, tested, and retested these recipes with large eggs so that they would work for you, since most of you are probably using large eggs.

If you are buying eggs at the farmers' market or collecting them from your own flock, they are probably not graded, but never fear. Pasta making is not rocket science. Far from it. Let's say that you have various-size eggs in the refrigerator and you still want to make pasta. Go ahead and use whichever eggs you have, and start with a little less flour. Add it in tablespoon by tablespoon until you reach the right dough consistency, which is soft and malleable, neither too stiff nor too sticky.

You may eventually find that you go so crazy for homemade pasta that you use hundreds of eggs a week and you can no longer justify buying so many eggs at the store because you get dirty looks from other patrons, and checkers have you on their *do not sell eggs to* lists, and so you're forced—strong-armed, really—to adopt some chickens, who will make you glorious, glorious eggs until the cows come home. Well, the cows will only come home if you adopt some of them, too, but you get the idea.

There are too many benefits to owning backyard birds for me to go into here, but one thing I will say with regard to pasta is that backyard birds tend to produce eggs with yolks richer and deeper yellow, bordering on orange, which makes for some spectacularly vibrant noodles. I was first lured into the fold (of a chicken's wing) when I was living in Piedmont, Italy, home of the cult-status pasta tajarin. When I laid eyes on those hand-cut, profoundly orange noodles, I knew that someday the universe would grant me the pleasure of calling a flock of birds my babes.

Be careful if you jump down the same nestbox hole, however, as there is this thing called "chicken math" that will get you every time. In essence, it's the inability to ever tell anyone the truth about how many birds you own, because you smuggle them into the flock any which way you can to the point that you purposefully lose count yourself. At printing, the author lives with ~~21 26 29 31~~ 33 chickens and ~~3 7~~ 13 ducks. That's her story and she's sticking to it.

ESPRESSO
You can't really make a pasta book while living in the Pacific Northwest with your heart still firmly ensconced in Torino, Italy, without tucking espresso in there somewhere. I do not partake in a daily dose of caffeine to fan my feathers, but that's not to say I don't love the flavor. As far as benefits are concerned, espresso is said to enhance long-term memory, increase focus, and lower your risk of both stroke and diabetes.

GOJI BERRIES
Goji berries are the fruits of the boxthorn tree, native to Asia. In pasta making, we use freeze-dried goji berries that have been pulverized into pretty orange powder. Goji berries are high in protein and contain eighteen different amino acids, plus more than twenty other trace minerals, including zinc, iron, phosphorus, and riboflavin.

Goji berries are also said to increase virility. There is an old saying in China that roughly translates to: *A man who goes on a long journey far from home should not take goji with him.*

HARISSA
My love for harissa bleeds orange, spicy, and deep. It's a North African spice paste that consists of various peppers and olive oil. The combination of peppers can vary regionally, and so can the heat intensity. You can make or purchase harissa. Trader Joe's sells a very good one that is vibrant and gorgeous in pasta. The capsaicin in the peppers has anti-inflammatory properties, plus it boosts metabolism and can really help clean you out, if you know what I mean. Of course we're not using so much here that you need to worry about your proximity to the loo.

LEAFY GREENS
Leafy greens are nutritional powerhouses that contain things like fiber, iron, magnesium, potassium, and calcium.

I never feel better than when I'm eating a bowlful of roughage. I know kale already had her moment in the sun, but she will live on in my heart and garden until my dying day. This book would not exist if it weren't for greens. They were the first thing I ever pureed into pasta, and dark green pasta remains among my favorite flavors.

In the spring and on into midsummer in many parts of the country, nettle season abounds. While they can be prickly and must be harvested with gloves, once boiled, they lose all their "sting." Nettle pasta is an earthy, lush green with a robust, minerally flavor. If you have occasion to harvest nettles, try using them to make Leafy Greens Dough (page 51) for something deliciously different.

MATCHA

I think of matcha, the highest quality powdered green tea available, as the Bob Marley of teas. You really can't hate it, even if you want to. I love the dusty green color and refined, subdued flavor it lends to pasta as much as or more than I love it in my mug on a cold winter's day. It's icing on the cake that matcha contains a potent class of antioxidants known as catechins, which aren't found in other foods and have cancer-fighting properties. Matcha is as calming as it is invigorating, and is said to fortify immunity, detoxification, and memory.

MILK AND CREAM

The milk dough in the book contains both milk and cream in just the right ratio to mimic the fat content of whole eggs. We've all probably seen a Got Milk? advertisement, which was one of the most successful and longest-running ad campaigns in history, but do we know why it's good for us? Milk is a rich source of calcium, which is necessary for bone and teeth health. Along with vitamin D, it helps prevent osteoporosis. The vitamin D in milk also supports serotonin production, thereby decreasing depression.

MOLE

Mole paste can be pretty controversial stuff unless you are making it yourself and you're an *abuela* from Mexico. Suffice it to say it's more than the sum of its parts, and if you think it's merely a Mexican savory chocolate sauce, you're mistaken. You can make it yourself in big batches and freeze it in ice cube trays, as I like to do, or you can buy a perfectly serviceable jar of it from nearly any grocery store shelf these days and no one will mind, especially if you're using it to flavor pasta dough. Since there are many variations, it's hard to make health claims about it generally, but peppers, chocolate, nuts, spices, and seeds tend to be in the mix, and those things in harmony are a pleasant, nutritious combination.

'NDUJA

My sweet meat tube lover, come here, will you? 'Nduja is a spicy Calabrian cured meat paste, which sounds all kinds of wrong, but is so, so right. If you haven't tried it and you're curious, think of it as spreadable prosciutto with a healthy, peppery kick. The peppers, in combination with the cured meat, bolster our metabolisms while teasing us with a protein spike that will boil the blood of virile pasta lovers the world over.

PAPRIKA

I first fell hard for paprika in Budapest, where I learned the difference between sweet, smoky, and spicy paprika after eating mounds and mounds of it in everything from *csirke* to goulash. Since then, I've swooned over Spanish paprika and hyperventilated over Hungarian, and I've yet to meet a paprika I didn't like, unless it was old. One important thing to consider when purchasing paprika is to buy it young as a nubile virgin, and don't keep it around past its pubescent prime. It loses its oomph faster than a grandpa coming off a three-day Viagra binge. It's an antioxidant-rich spice that fights disease, is anti-inflammatory, and is especially high in beta-carotene.

PARSLEY

Roman scholar Pliny the Elder wrote that all people love parsley. Maybe we need to plant more parsley farms and somehow use it to unite the masses? Because it's difficult to grow, it's said that only witches or evil people can manage it, and while I think of myself as something of a witch, I sadly lack the green thumb for parsley.

Parsley is an immunity booster and breath-freshener, is rich in vitamins A, K, C, and others, and is a good source of volatile compounds such as myristicin.

PEAS

My two favorite facts about peas, if you please, are these:

One serving of peas contains as much vitamin C as two large apples, more fiber than a slice of wheat bread, and more thiamine than a pint of wheat.

It is estimated that more than nine thousand peas are eaten per person, per year in Britain.

POPPY SEEDS

Be mindful if you're eating one of the gnudi or sauce recipes in this book that feature poppy seeds and traveling to Singapore soon after, as they're a prohibited substance there, probably because they contain opium alkaloids, which when ingested can give false readings in a drug test. They're actually pretty innocent and nutritionally loaded, however. Chia seeds are all the rage, but good old poppy seeds boast healthier amounts of thiamine, folate, and several essential minerals, including calcium, iron, magnesium, manganese, phosphorus, and zinc.

PURPLE SWEET POTATOES

The specific purple sweet potato called for in this book is a variety called Stokes. It has a much deeper purple color and a drier texture than any other purple sweet potato, which makes it the right choice for gnocchi. A good source of vitamin C, Stokes Purple has the most anthocyanins, the antioxidant compound in the purple pigments, of all three purple sweet potatoes. The color intensifies when cooked, making for the prettiest purple dumplings you ever did see.

SPIRULINA

Blue Majik (no, that's not a typo) spirulina is a proprietary, chemical-free extract of standard green spirulina, which you might know as the powder that turns smoothies green. Blue Majik has a cerulean blue pigment that contains both phycocyanin and non-PC compounds. This combination is not seen in standard spirulina powder, and it's what gives it the specific blue shade. It's somewhat pricy to purchase a 50-gram bottle of the fine powder (available through E3Live, on Amazon, or other health food stores, both online and physical), but a little bit goes a long way. Be sure and buy it in fine powder form, as capsules would be difficult to work with in pasta dough. It will keep well stored in an airtight container in the refrigerator.

TOMATOES

Did you know that the scientific name for tomato is *Solanum lycopersicum*, and that *lycopersicum* means "wolf peach"? Why can't we just call them wolf peaches from now on? It's so much more memorable. Tomatoes contain all four major carotenoids: alpha- and beta-carotene, lutein, and lycopene. These carotenoids have individual benefits, but, like the X-Men, they work better as a group. In particular, tomatoes contain tremendous amounts of lycopene, thought to have the highest antioxidant activity of all the carotenoids.

TURMERIC

Note that there is an *r* in the middle of the word *turmeric*. Personally, I'm a fan of pronouncing it as such, and whenever I hear *toomuric* I think that person engages in *too* much baby talk.

Curcumin is the bright yellow pigment and active ingredient in turmeric. It has powerful antioxidant and anti-inflammatory properties. Turmeric requires heat and piperine (black pepper) to increase its absorption. It's also fat-soluble, which means it dissolves in fat. So in order to maximize turmeric's health benefits, cook it, serve it with some kind of fat (butter), and lay on the black pepper. For a good time, sheet the Parsley-Pepper-Turmeric Dough on page 50 into noodles and serve it with the Thyme Browned Butter on page 203.

1

DOUGH

THE DOS AND DON'TS OF DOUGH

Pasta. For something so straightforward, there sure are plenty of different opinions on how to make it. For every shape, a Google search will yield a hundred different recipes, and you may be left scratching your head as to why. To get to the truth of the matter, examine the far corners of your pasta soul and answer one question: How do *you* like it? Once you've figured that out, you can make the necessary adjustments in how you prepare it to suit your own taste. Personally, I like it supple, vibrant,

al dente (literally, "to the tooth" in Italian), and never mushy. I developed the dough formulas, resting times, sheeting instructions, and cooking times with those preferences in mind. I also based the batches of dough on what will fit comfortably through a standard at-home pasta machine, such as an Atlas.

One significant divergence you'll see with the dough in this book as compared with countless other pasta recipes out there is the sole inclusion of "00" pasta flour over semolina flour. "00" (double zero or *doppio zero*) pasta flour is a low-gluten, finely milled flour that is soft, malleable, and very easy to work with.

Because most of the doughs herein go on to become shapes that are sometimes complicated and often multicolored by the time they're done, I needed the dough to be as foolproof to work with as possible, and to not dry out easily during the sheeting and shaping process. The dough that results from "00" pasta flour is easier to work with than semolina-based dough, which is stiffer and drier.

You are welcome to substitute a portion of the flour for semolina; just note that you will want to take extra precautions to keep your dough covered and potentially rehydrate it with a water spray bottle adjusted to the finest mist setting. As you become speedier and more proficient at weaving together colors and shapes, adding semolina flour to your pasta dough will give it the leathery parchment quality that sets Italian pasta apart from other noodles. If you want to give this a try, start with substituting ½ cup per standard recipe.

Even if you never wish to use it in your pasta dough, I recommend keeping semolina flour on hand for two important uses. First, it's useful to dust surfaces you plan to store pasta on with semolina so that the pasta doesn't stick to the surface or itself. Second, any of the sauce recipes that call for hot pasta water need the help of an extra handful of semolina to become starchy enough to add that viscous quality that elevates pasta sauce from good to great (see "Semolina Starchiness," page 67).

Let's revisit "00" pasta flour for a moment. Italian flour is milled on a scale from coarse to fine. The coarsest flour is "2" and the finest flour is "000." Imagine holding a handful of bran in your palm— thick and rough, right? Now empty your palm and pour onto it a few ounces of cornstarch. It's soft, smooth, almost weightless. "000" milling results in flour about as fine as cornstarch, and is quite rare, even in Italy.

This degree of coarseness has nothing to do with the percentage of protein in the flour. Higher-protein flours are valued for baking, especially sourdough baking, when long fermentation times develop more flavor in the resulting bread, pizza, or baked good. Fresh pasta, on the other hand, is at its very best when the protein content of the flour is lower, resulting in a more delicate noodle. Higher-protein flour results in tough noodles that fracture easily.

It's very important to note these two different scales when considering "00" flour, because a flour can be "00" with either high or low protein. Italian mills distinguish "00 Pizza Flour" from "00 Pasta Flour," and that distinction ultimately refers to the protein content.

In short, don't use "00 Pizza Flour" to make pasta. If you cannot find "00 Pasta Flour," feel free to substitute all-purpose flour, and bonus points if you can find one with a lower protein content. As the United States is fast catching up with the rest of the world in establishing a firm food culture, more domestic millers are labeling protein content on their bags of flour. So here's what to look for in flour: *low protein, finely milled.*

That being said, all of these recipes will work with plain old all-purpose flour. Don't stress too much—it's pasta making, so sip a glass of wine and relax.

If you really want to nail the flour in your pasta recipes, these are available domestically and will work the very best:

MOLINI PIVETTI SFOGLIA GOLD ROSA 00. This is formulated specifically for pasta. Bonus—it comes in 5-kilogram bags and isn't very pricy if you can find it. In Seattle, it's available at Big John's PFI. These recipes were developed using this flour, and then retested using all-purpose (AP) flour and Caputo. The texture of noodles using Rosa "00" is ethereal—I can promise you'll love them.

BARILLA FARINA "00". This is a lower-protein "00" flour that works well for pasta and is available at Guidi Marcello in Santa Monica, California. Guidi Marcello is a Mecca destination for me. If you can't make it there in person, they also ship.

ANTICO MOLLINO CAPUTO "00" PASTA FRESCA & GNOCCHI FLOUR. Fifty-five-pound bags, available on Amazon, shipped to

your door? What's not to love? It's about $100 a bag including shipping, but that works out to $1.82 a pound, which is a small price to pay for perfect pasta.

CENTRAL MILLING ORGANIC TYPE 00 NORMAL. Not as high in protein as their reinforced "00," this flour is soft yet structured. I love that it's organic and domestic. Central Milling is my favorite domestic mill for their attention to quality and detail and true commitment to the craft of flour milling.

ANSON MILLS PASTA MAKER'S FLOUR. Really expensive, but when you read about their milling technique and grain sourcing (described on their website), it suddenly seems worth it. When I make pasta with this flour, I pretend I'm cooking a fancy dinner for Elton John and Queen Elizabeth and then I can justify the cost.

KING ARTHUR ITALIAN-STYLE FLOUR. This is a low-gluten, soft flour made by one of our country's preeminent sources of quality grain products. I wish it came in larger bags, but it's nevertheless worth a mention as it's supple, smooth, and easy to work with.

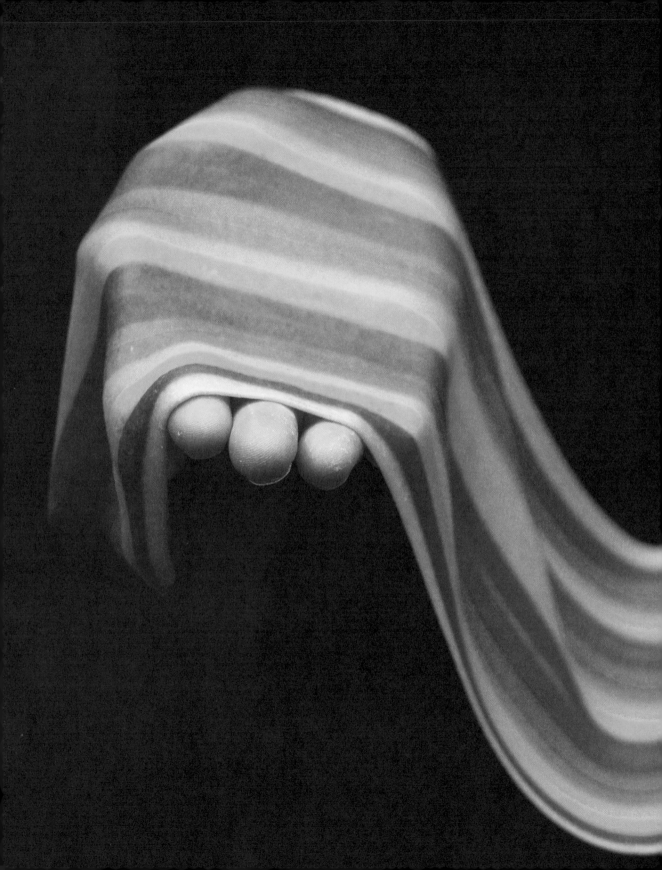

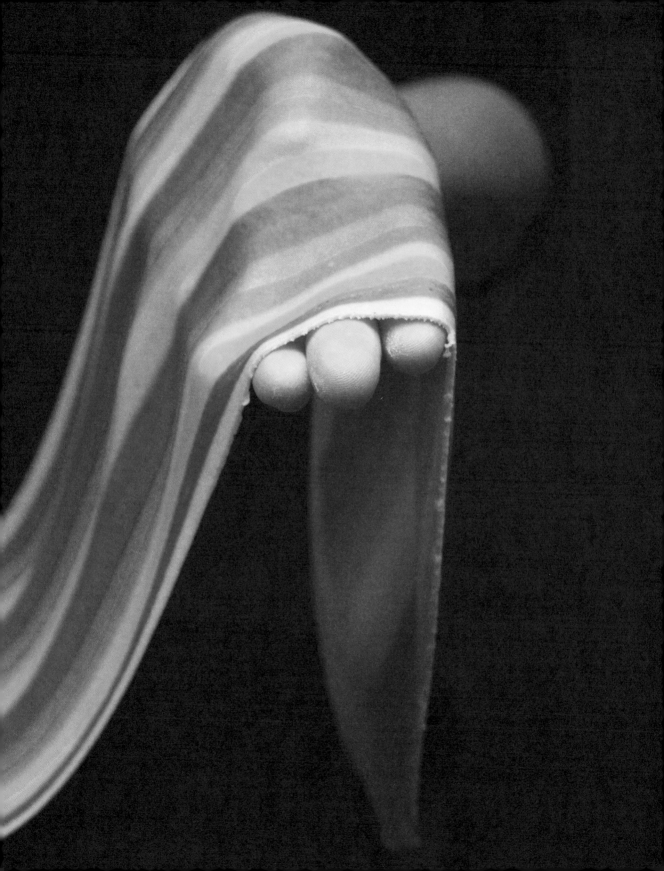

MAKING SOFTER COLORS

As you dive into creating colored dough, you will see that the process is much the same for each one, and usually involves making a puree of eggs mixed with a colorful ingredient (except the few water-based doughs), then adding that to flour.

I developed the recipes here with flavor and color intensity in mind, and as such, most of the colors are strong, pure versions of themselves. If you wanted to make pastels or other softer colors, you can easily do that by adding less of the flavor ingredient. For example, the Red Beet Dough on page 39 calls for

1 medium beet. If you wanted a pale pink, you could add 2 tablespoons chopped beet instead. To determine the final dough color outcome, look at the shade of the puree after you've blended it. The dough will most closely resemble the color of the puree, so if you want it lighter or darker, add less or more of the flavor ingredient.

STAND MIXER OR FOOD PROCESSOR?

While the dough recipes were designed to be made with a stand mixer, if you have a large, high-powered food

processor, you can use that as well. If you're using a food processor, make sure to add the flour first, then the colored puree (or plain eggs or water-based color). Pulse until the dough starts to come together, then use the continuous "on" function to whiz the dough into a ball. Note that the food processor blade does a thorough job of cutting the liquid into the flour and can result in sticky dough. This is easily remedied by tossing in extra flour a handful at a time until the dough resembles silky Play-Doh.

Unless you don't mind big chunks in your dough, resist the urge to make the colored puree directly in the food processor, as it does not homogenize as evenly as it does in the blender.

EGG-FREE DOUGH

While a couple of the doughs in this book are naturally egg-free because mixing eggs with the flavor ingredient would ruin the color outcome, every dough *can* be made egg-free with a quick adjustment. This is welcome news for vegan readers and anyone who is allergic to or avoiding eggs. While I am smitten with my chickens and ducks and I love the eggs they provide me, I'm not sure I would eat quite so egg-heavily if I didn't implicitly trust my source.

To make egg-free pasta dough, replace the eggs in any of the recipes with ¾ cup hot tap water. If you're

making plain dough, you can add this directly to the flour, or if you're experimenting with colored dough, add the water to the blender along with the flavor ingredient. You may need to adjust the final dough by adding a spoonful or two more water or flour to achieve the exact Play-Doh consistency you're after, but this will give you a good idea of where to start.

The texture of egg-free dough is tackier, making it slightly harder to work with, but it won't take long to get the hang of it.

A SPECTRUM OF POSSIBILITIES

As I've been writing this book, I've received hundreds of messages from parents of autistic children, asking either how to purchase colorful pasta or how to make it. It opened my eyes to many of the sensory and nutritional issues people on the autism spectrum face. While making vegetable-dyed noodles at home is not for everyone, it may be a fun activity to try with or for kids with autism. There is no one-size-fits-all approach to sensory processing disorders, but many parents have told me that they seek out specific hues and texturally varied foods that don't contain artificial dyes or flavors. I hope this book can provide a wealth of recipes that fit the bill.

THE DOUGHS

Each dough recipe makes about 18 ounces of dough, or four 4½-ounce portions. The doughs generally last 3 days in the fridge, though oxidation may cause them to either fade or intensify in color over time. (See page 78 for information on drying and freezing pasta.)

RED BEET DOUGH

PINK

I've made it a life mission of mine to convert beet haters to beet lovers, and this dough is an excellent place to start. The beet flavor is really subtle if you can taste it at all, and the color is so striking, what's not to love? If color is your primary motivating factor for making this dough, consider using frozen beets. Since more of the water content is removed from the beet upon freezing, it yields a very consistently vibrant color.

1 medium beet (about 4 ounces), peeled and roughly chopped
  (or use 4 ounces frozen beet chunks)
2 large eggs
2½ cups "00" pasta flour

1. Put the beet in a small, non-metal bowl and cover with plastic wrap. Microwave for 50 seconds. Let sit for 2 minutes. Uncover and put in a blender along with the eggs. Mix on low speed to combine, slowly increasing speed until a smooth puree forms.

2. Combine the flour and puree in the bowl of a standing mixer fitted with a paddle attachment and mix on low speed until a ball of dough forms. Continue to knead for 3 minutes, either by hand or in the mixer, so that the dough develops elasticity and silkiness. Cover the ball of dough in plastic wrap and let it rest at room temperature for 30 minutes before sheeting (see page 80).

3. Alternatively, you can let the dough rest for up to 24 hours in the refrigerator. The dough will turn reddish brown after that, although it's still usable for up to 3 days.

BEET-BLUEBERRY DOUGH
PERFECT PURPLE

This dough comes out Prince (RIP) purple. It's colorfast and extra smooth, although keep in mind that the blueberry seeds give it tiny, charming flecks. Frozen blueberries yield a slightly richer purple color, but either fresh or frozen blueberries will work fine.

1 small beet (about 2 ounces), peeled and roughly chopped
(or use 2 ounces frozen beet chunks; see page 21)
¼ cup fresh or frozen blueberries
2 large eggs
2¼ cups "OO" pasta flour

1. Put the beet in a small, non-metal bowl and cover with plastic wrap. Microwave for 50 seconds. Let sit for 2 minutes. Uncover and add to a blender along with the blueberries and eggs and blend on low speed to combine, slowly increasing speed until a smooth puree forms.

2. Combine the flour and puree in the bowl of a standing mixer fitted with a paddle attachment and mix on low speed until a ball of dough forms. Continue to knead for 3 minutes, either by hand or in the mixer, so that the dough develops elasticity and silkiness. Cover the ball of dough in plastic wrap and let it rest at room temperature for 30 minutes before sheeting (see page 80).

3. Alternatively, you can let the dough rest for up to 24 hours in the refrigerator. The color will turn grayish brown after that, although the dough is still usable for up to 3 days.

BLUEBERRY DOUGH
GRAYISH LAVENDER

This dough is more on the dusty lavender side of purple. It can be tacky compared with some of the other doughs in these pages, so add extra flour if the tackiness borders on sticky. The benefit of that is it's a very malleable dough that's easy to work with, and you can sheet it without a pasta machine if need be. Because of this and its appealing scent and color, make this one to entice kids into joining the kitchen fun. Note that any sweetness present in the dough tends to disappear when cooked and served with sauce.

¾ cup frozen blueberries
2 large eggs
2¼ cups "00" pasta flour

1. In a blender, mix the blueberries and eggs on low speed, slowly increasing speed until a smooth puree forms.

2. Combine the flour and puree in the bowl of a standing mixer fitted with a paddle attachment and mix on low speed until a ball of dough forms. Continue to knead for 3 minutes, either by hand or in the mixer, so that the dough develops elasticity and silkiness. Cover the ball of dough in plastic wrap and let it rest at room temperature for 30 minutes before sheeting (see page 80).

3. Alternatively, you can let the dough rest for up to 24 hours in the refrigerator. The dough will turn gray after that, although it's still usable for up to 3 days.

BUCKWHEAT DOUGH
SPECKLED TAN

Buckwheat is actually a seed, not a grass like wheat (see page 21). When it's milled into flour, it resembles wheat, but it performs very differently and lends a pleasant nuttiness to dough. Pasta made from this dough plays nicely and looks phenomenal with Matcha Dough (page 52).

1¾ cups "00" pasta flour
½ cup buckwheat flour
2 large eggs
⅓ cup hot water

1. Combine the flours, eggs, and hot water in the bowl of a standing mixer fitted with a paddle attachment and mix on low speed until a ball of dough forms. Continue to knead for 3 minutes, either by hand or in the mixer, so that the dough develops elasticity and silkiness. Cover the ball of dough in plastic wrap and let it rest at room temperature for 30 minutes before sheeting (see page 80).

2. Alternatively, you can let the dough rest for up to 24 hours in the refrigerator. The color sometimes intensifies after that, although the dough is still usable for up to 3 days.

ACTIVATED CHARCOAL DOUGH

BLACK

Activated charcoal can be found easily online and in many health food stores. This is the dough I make whenever I'm thinking about line drawing on sheets of pasta with actual spaghetti-thin pasta noodles. Black is a surprisingly important color to have in your wheelhouse of vibrant dough because it helps to define the bright colors and makes them stand out. It's also a fun dough to turn into noodles all on its own or layered with orange around Halloween.

> 2 tablespoons activated charcoal powder
> 4 large eggs
> 2¼ cups "00" pasta flour

1. In a blender, mix the charcoal, eggs, and 1 teaspoon water on low speed, slowly increasing speed until a smooth puree forms.

2. Combine the flour and puree in the bowl of a standing mixer fitted with a paddle attachment and mix on low speed until a ball of dough forms. Continue to knead for 3 minutes, either by hand or in the mixer, so that the dough develops elasticity and silkiness. Cover the ball of dough in plastic wrap and let it rest at room temperature for 30 minutes before sheeting (see page 80).

3. Alternatively, you can let the dough rest for up to 24 hours in the refrigerator. The color deepens after that, although the dough is still usable for up to 3 days.

SPIRULINA DOUGH
LIGHTER BLUE

Blue Majik is a specially formulated spirulina that isolates the C-phycocyanin, which is rich in antioxidants with anti-inflammatory properties. It's also what makes it much more blue than other spirulina, and why it's the only choice for making this lighter blue shade of pasta. This shade will fade when cooked for too long, so use it to make thin, fresh noodles that only kiss the boiling water for seconds. It's somewhat pricy, but a little bit goes a long way. Be sure to buy it in fine powder form, as capsules won't work in pasta dough.

2¼ cups "00" pasta flour
1 tablespoon fine Blue Majik spirulina powder
¾ cup hot water

1. Combine the flour and spirulina in the bowl of a standing mixer fitted with a paddle attachment and mix on low speed for 15 seconds. Pour in the hot water and mix on low speed until a ball of dough forms. Continue to knead for 3 minutes, either by hand or in the mixer, so that the dough develops elasticity and silkiness. Cover the ball of dough in plastic wrap and let it rest at room temperature for 30 minutes before sheeting (see page 80).

2. Alternatively, you can let the dough rest for up to 24 hours in the refrigerator. The color sometimes darkens after that, although the dough is still usable for up to 3 days.

BUTTERFLY PEA FLOWER DOUGH
BLUE

Butterfly pea flower dough is a regal shade of unmistakable blue it's hard to believe exists in nature, and yet it does. This recipe, like many in the book, is easily tweakable. You can adjust the hue as if on a sliding scale by adding a little bit of baking soda for a blue that veers toward green or a little bit of vinegar to get a more purple dough. I would not add more than ½ teaspoon baking soda or 1 tablespoon vinegar, because you'll throw off the taste and texture, not to mention the ratio of ingredients.

This is a water-based dough for a reason. When you mix too many yellow egg yolks with butterfly pea flowers, you'll wind up with a muddy, unattractive green-blue.

Butterfly pea flowers can be readily sourced online—Amazon has a constantly changing selection of vendors, so I usually purchase from the one that's most highly rated at the time of my search.

1 cup boiling water
Packed ½ cup dried butterfly pea flowers
2¼ cups "00" pasta flour

1. Combine the boiling water and flowers in a bowl and stir to make sure all flowers are submerged. Let steep for 10 minutes, then press the steeped mixture through a strainer directly into the bowl of a standing mixer containing the flour. Depending how well you pressed the flowers, you may need to add a touch more flour to this dough, as it can be on the sticky side. You may not need quite all of the steeped liquid, but be sure to reserve any extra by pressing it into a separate liquid measuring cup in case you do.

2. Fit the mixer with a paddle attachment and mix on low speed until a ball of dough forms. Continue to knead for 3 minutes, either by hand or in the mixer, so that the dough develops elasticity and silkiness. Cover the ball of dough in plastic wrap and let it rest at room temperature for 30 minutes before sheeting (see page 80).

3. Alternatively, you can let the dough rest for up to 24 hours in the refrigerator. The color sometimes intensifies after that, although the dough is still usable for up to 3 days.

CACAO DOUGH
RICH BROWN

Surprisingly enough, pasta made with the inclusion of cocoa powder has a longstanding, if not widely known, tradition in Italy. Historically, it was served with only *dolce-forte* or sweet and spicy sauce, because the strong flavor of the cocoa is difficult to pair with anything else. I use cacao instead of cocoa both because it's healthier and because the flavor is subtle and on the cusp of sweet and savory, so the noodles are more easily paired with sauce.

Incidentally, chocolate in pasta existed in Italy before chocolate in dessert. Italians use chocolate in dessert only to adorn cakes, not inside of them, because the flavor of chocolate is considered too heavy for the lighter touch of Italian pastry.

This dough is remarkably easy to work with and is a striking shade of mahogany. You can add more or less cacao powder depending how deep you want your brown to be. The dough sheeted into pasta works very well with richer meat sauces, such as the Pollo Agrodolce on page 239.

2¼ cups "00" pasta flour
2 tablespoons cacao powder
4 large eggs

1. Combine the flour and cacao powder in the bowl of a standing mixer fitted with a paddle attachment and mix on medium speed for 1 minute. Add the eggs and mix on low speed until a ball of dough forms. Continue to knead for 3 minutes, either by hand or in the mixer, so that the dough develops elasticity and silkiness. Cover the ball of dough in plastic wrap and let it rest at room temperature for 30 minutes before sheeting (see page 80).

2. Alternatively, you can let the dough rest for up to 24 hours in the refrigerator. The color sometimes intensifies after that, although the dough is still usable for up to 3 days.

MOLE DOUGH
SILKY BROWN

Once a year, I make a big batch of mole paste and freeze it. It's a bit of effort, but I make enough to last for a while and pre-portion it in an ice cube tray. You certainly don't need to go to all that trouble to make this pasta dough, however, as a jar of mole from the supermarket will yield pasta that is rich and savory with a subtle chocolaty flavor that is hard to beat. Mole pasta complements cream sauces as well as rich or spicy meat sugos. I am very fond of making filled pasta such as agnolotti using mole pasta sheets and Taleggio Pear Filling (page 257).

1/3 cup mole paste
2 large eggs
2¼ cups "00" pasta flour

1. In a blender, mix the mole and eggs on low speed, slowly increasing speed until a smooth puree forms.

2. Combine the flour and puree in the bowl of a standing mixer fitted with a paddle attachment and mix on low speed until a ball of dough forms. Continue to knead for 3 minutes, either by hand or in the mixer, so that the dough develops elasticity and silkiness. Cover the ball of dough in plastic wrap and let it rest at room temperature for 30 minutes before sheeting (see page 80).

3. Alternatively, you can let the dough rest for up to 24 hours in the refrigerator. The color sometimes intensifies after that, although the dough is still usable for up to 3 days.

CHESTNUT DOUGH

WARM BROWN

Chestnuts and pasta go hand in hand in Italy, often appearing in gnocchi, ravioli, and sauces. I opted to incorporate chestnut flour directly into the dough because the delicate nuttiness it lends is complementary to a diverse variety of sauces, such as Pollo Agrodolce (page 257), any of the browned butters, or on the lighter side, even Cold Noodle Dipping Sauce (page 224). Resist the urge to increase the ratio of chestnut to pasta flour even if you really love chestnut, as too much makes for an excessively gummy dough.

1¾ cups "00" pasta flour
⅓ cup chestnut flour
4 large eggs

1. Combine the flours and eggs in the bowl of a standing mixer fitted with a paddle attachment and mix on low speed until a ball of dough forms. Continue to knead for 3 minutes, either by hand or in the mixer, so that the dough develops elasticity and silkiness. Cover the ball of dough in plastic wrap and let it rest at room temperature for 30 minutes before sheeting (see page 80).

2. Alternatively, you can let the dough rest for up to 24 hours in the refrigerator. The color sometimes intensifies after that, although the dough is still usable for up to 3 days.

PEA DOUGH
LIGHT GREEN

This pastel green dough has a very approachable flavor that is a big hit with everyone who tries it. Bonus: Most of us have the ingredients on hand for pea dough at any given time. If you want to make it a little more chartreuse, you can experiment with adding either 1 teaspoon ground turmeric or 1 inch peeled and chopped fresh turmeric root (see page 29).

½ cup frozen peas, thawed at room temperature for at least 10 minutes
3 large eggs
1 scant tablespoon hot water
2¼ cups "00" pasta flour

1. In a blender, mix the peas, eggs, and hot water on low speed, slowly increasing speed until a smooth puree forms.

2. Combine the flour and puree in the bowl of a standing mixer fitted with a paddle attachment and mix on low speed until a ball of dough forms. Continue to knead for 3 minutes, either by hand or in the mixer, so that the dough develops elasticity and silkiness. Cover the ball of dough in plastic wrap and let it rest at room temperature for 30 minutes before sheeting (see page 80).

3. Alternatively, you can let the dough rest for up to 24 hours in the refrigerator. The color sometimes fades after that, although the dough is still usable for up to 3 days.

PARSLEY-PEPPER-TURMERIC DOUGH
SPECKLED CHARTREUSE GREEN

I'm a big, big fan of the color chartreuse, and this dough is close to that shade, with flattering smatters of black accenting the green. It's no accident that I included black pepper, since the active ingredient in black pepper, piperine, is said to increase the body's absorption of the curcumin in turmeric. Health benefits aside, make this dough just once for me, pretty please, since I'm so partial to its gorgeous color.

1 tablespoon kosher salt
1 teaspoon baking soda
1 bunch fresh parsley
1 inch fresh turmeric root, peeled and chopped; or ½ teaspoon
    ground turmeric
½ teaspoon freshly ground black pepper
2 large eggs
2¼ cups "00" pasta flour

1. In a large saucepan over high heat, bring the salt, baking soda, and 8 cups water to a boil. Add the parsley and blanch it for 15 seconds. Drain and press out the water.

2. Add the parsley to a blender and wait 1 or 2 minutes for it to cool. Add the turmeric, pepper, and eggs and blend on low speed at first to combine, then increase the speed and puree until smooth.

3. Strain the puree with a fine-mesh sieve over a small bowl to remove and discard any grainy threads.

4. In the bowl of a standing mixer fitted with a paddle attachment, combine the flour and puree. Mix on low speed until a ball of dough forms. Continue to knead for 3 minutes, either by hand or in the mixer, so that the dough develops elasticity and silkiness. Cover the ball of dough in plastic wrap and let it rest at room temperature for 30 minutes before sheeting (page 80).

5. Alternatively, you can let the dough rest for up to 24 hours in the refrigerator. The color sometimes intensifies after that, although the dough is still usable for up to 3 days.

LEAFY GREENS DOUGH

DARK GREEN

This is a rich dough with wonderfully deep color. Lacinato kale is my go-to dark, leafy green, but others such as spinach or chard are great too. It's fun to see the subtle variations in color if you get a chance to make three or four different leafy green doughs at once.

In spring, when nettles lie in treacherous wait along all my running trails, I love to use them instead, as a little bit of payback for all the times they've stung me. They're considered a superfood, and among other claims to fame, they contain twenty-nine times more calcium than spinach. Wear gloves when harvesting nettles and use only the tender leaves from the top 2 inches of the plant. For this recipe I use about 4 cups packed fresh nettle leaves. After they are blanched, you can touch them with bare hands without getting stung.

1 tablespoon kosher salt
1 teaspoon baking soda
½ bunch lacinato kale or other dark leafy greens, such as spinach
    (4 to 6 ounces, or about 2 packed cups baby spinach) or nettles
2 large eggs
2¼ cups "00" pasta flour

1. In a large saucepan over high heat, bring the salt, baking soda, and 8 cups water to a boil. Add the kale and blanch it for 15 seconds. Strain and press out the water.

2. Add the kale to a blender and wait 1 or 2 minutes for it to cool. Add the eggs and blend on low speed at first to combine, then increase the speed and puree until smooth.

3. Strain the puree with a fine-mesh sieve over a small bowl to remove and discard any grainy threads. This should yield about 1 cup puree.

4. In the bowl of a standing mixer fitted with a paddle attachment, combine the flour and puree. Mix on low speed until a ball of dough forms. Continue to knead for 3 minutes, either by hand or in the mixer, so that the dough develops elasticity and silkiness. Cover the ball of dough in plastic wrap and let it rest at room temperature for 30 minutes before sheeting (see page 80).

5. Alternatively, you can let the dough rest for up to 24 hours in the refrigerator. The color sometimes intensifies after that, although the dough is still usable for up to 3 days.

MATCHA DOUGH
DUSTY GREEN

Matcha, or green tea powder, is beloved the world over for both its unmistakable dusty green color and its complex and alluring taste. It looks fantastic paired with cacao or turmeric dough when making any of the two-sided pastas detailed in the sheeting designs that start on page 96. Look for culinary matcha as opposed to drinking (or artisanal) matcha for use in cooking. Culinary matcha is less expensive, and boiling water destroys the amino acid structures in drinking matcha, so you would lose the delicate flavor nuances of that fancier matcha anyway.

1 tablespoon plus 1 teaspoon culinary matcha powder
3 large eggs
⅓ cup hot water
2¼ cups "00" pasta flour

1. In a blender, mix the matcha, eggs, and water on low speed, slowly increasing speed until a smooth puree forms.

2. Combine the flour and puree in the bowl of a standing mixer fitted with a paddle attachment and mix on low speed until a ball of dough forms. Continue to knead for 3 minutes, either by hand or in the mixer, so that the dough develops elasticity and silkiness. Cover the ball of dough in plastic wrap and let it rest at room temperature for 30 minutes before sheeting (see page 80).

3. Alternatively, you can let the dough rest for up to 24 hours in the refrigerator. The color sometimes intensifies after that, although the dough is still usable for up to 3 days.

AÇAI DOUGH
MARBLED BROWNISH BLACK

Açai dough yields a dark, supple, textured noodle. I like to combine sheeted açai dough with blueberry beet dough for an antioxidant powerhouse pasta that goes very well with Golden Milk Ragù (page 236). Açai is available freeze-dried at most natural foods retailers, such as Whole Foods.

2 tablespoons açai powder
4 large eggs
2¼ cups "00" flour

1. In a blender, mix the açai and eggs on low speed to combine, slowly increasing speed until a smooth puree forms.

2. Combine the flour and puree in the bowl of a standing mixer fitted with a paddle attachment and mix on low speed until a ball of dough forms. Continue to knead for 3 minutes, either by hand or in the mixer, so that the dough develops elasticity and silkiness. Cover the ball of dough in plastic wrap and let it rest at room temperature for 30 minutes before sheeting (see page 80).

3. Alternatively, you can let the dough rest for up to 24 hours in the refrigerator. The color sometimes fades or intensifies after that, although the dough is still usable for up to 3 days.

MILK DOUGH
WHITE

This dough is as close as you can get to white pasta without using unnatural ingredients. It has the added benefit of being smooth, supple, and easy to sheet. It's about the best dough I can think of for chicken noodle soup, especially when it's cut into wide, pappardelle-style noodles. Don't try adding eggs unless you want the dough to yellow. The combination of milk and cream is meant to mimic the fat content in an egg without the pigment of the yolk.

> 2¼ cups "00" pasta flour, or more as needed
> ½ cup whole milk, or more as needed
> ⅓ cup heavy cream

1. Combine the flour, milk, and cream in the bowl of a standing mixer fitted with a paddle attachment and mix on low speed until the dough starts to come together. If it's a touch on the dry side, add a tablespoon or two more milk, and if it's too sticky, a bit more flour will firm it up. Continue to knead for 3 minutes, either by hand or in the mixer, so that the dough develops elasticity and silkiness. Cover the ball of dough in plastic wrap and let it rest at room temperature for 30 minutes before sheeting (see page 80).

2. Alternatively, you can let the dough rest for up to 24 hours in the refrigerator. The color sometimes yellows after that, although the dough is still usable for up to 3 days.

BASIC MOTHER DOUGH
PALE YELLOW

This dough is the real workhorse of the bunch. It's classic pale yellow and extremely versatile. If you've never made pasta before, this is the best place to start.

2¼ cups "00" pasta flour
4 large eggs

1. Combine the flour and eggs in the bowl of a standing mixer fitted with a paddle attachment and mix on low speed until a ball of dough forms. Continue to knead for 3 minutes, either by hand or in the mixer, so that the dough develops elasticity and silkiness. Cover the ball of dough in plastic wrap and let it rest at room temperature for 30 minutes before sheeting (see page 80).

2. Alternatively, you can let the dough rest for up to 24 hours in the refrigerator. The color sometimes fades after that, although the dough is still usable for up to 3 days.

TURMERIC DOUGH
BRIGHT YELLOW

Not all turmeric is created equal. If you can find fresh turmeric root, you won't regret using it, because your dough will be the brightest yellow. If you can only source ground turmeric, look at every brand in the store and choose based on the color you wish your dough to become, as some are more mustardy and some are sunshiny bright.

In order to maximize the health benefits of turmeric, it should be served with both black pepper and fat of some sort, which makes pasta made with this dough a candidate for Pecorino-Pepper Sauce with Broccolini (page 219).

> 3 inches fresh turmeric root, peeled and chopped;
>   or 1 tablespoon ground turmeric
> 4 large eggs
> 2¼ cups "00" pasta flour

1. In a blender, mix the turmeric and eggs on low speed to combine, slowly increasing speed until a smooth puree forms.

2. Combine the flour and puree in the bowl of a standing mixer fitted with a paddle attachment and mix on low speed until a ball of dough forms. Continue to knead for 3 minutes, either by hand or in the mixer, so that the dough develops elasticity and silkiness. Cover the ball of dough in plastic wrap and let it rest at room temperature for 30 minutes before sheeting (see page 80).

3. Alternatively, you can let the dough rest for up to 24 hours in the refrigerator. The dough develops dark flecks after that, although it's still usable for up to 3 days.

GOJI BERRY DOUGH
PALE ORANGE

My acupuncturist got me permanently hooked on goji berries, which is a rarity for me, because usually when people recommend supplements I take them for a week and then forget them. I stuck with goji berries because I love their tart, sweet, slightly herbal taste, and I'm nothing if not flavor-driven. Look for ready-made goji berry powder rather than trying to pulverize your own. Just picture what would happen to your blender or food processor if you tried to powder raisins.

¼ cup freeze-dried goji berry powder
4 large eggs
2½ cups "00" pasta flour

1. In a blender, mix the goji berry powder and eggs on low speed to combine, slowly increasing speed until a smooth puree forms.

2. Combine the flour and puree in the bowl of a standing mixer fitted with a paddle attachment and mix on low speed until a ball of dough forms. Continue to knead for 3 minutes, either by hand or in the mixer, so that the dough develops elasticity and silkiness. Cover the ball of dough in plastic wrap and let it rest at room temperature for 30 minutes before sheeting (see page 80).

3. Alternatively, you can let the dough rest for up to 24 hours in the refrigerator. The color sometimes fades or intensifies after that, although the dough is still usable for up to 3 days.

CARROT DOUGH

PALE ORANGE, VEERING TOWARD ORANGE-YELLOW, BUT STILL ORANGE

This dough sheeted into pasta is versatile and relatively neutral in flavor. It also makes very good chilled noodles that pair well with Cold Noodle Dipping Sauce (page 224).

2¼ cups "00" pasta flour
¾ cup fresh 100 percent carrot juice

1. Combine the flour and carrot juice in the bowl of a standing mixer fitted with a paddle attachment and mix on low speed until a ball of dough forms. Continue to knead for 3 minutes, either by hand or in the mixer, so that the dough develops elasticity and silkiness. Cover the ball of dough in plastic wrap and let it rest at room temperature for 30 minutes before sheeting (see page 80).

2. Alternatively, you can let the dough rest for up to 24 hours in the refrigerator. The color sometimes fades or intensifies after that, although the dough is still usable for up to 3 days.

TOMATO DOUGH
LIGHT ORANGE

This dough relies on tomato paste rather than fresh or sauced tomatoes, because the concentrate lends a stronger flavor and greater color intensity. It's a very aromatic dough, so if you love tomatoes you can amp that up further by serving it with Fast, Fresh Tomato Sauce with Ricotta Salata (page 209).

2¼ cups "00" pasta flour
3 large eggs
¼ cup tomato paste

1. Combine the flour, eggs, and tomato paste in the bowl of a standing mixer fitted with a paddle attachment and mix on low speed until a ball of dough forms. Continue to knead for 3 minutes, either by hand or in the mixer, so that the dough develops elasticity and silkiness. Cover the ball of dough in plastic wrap and let it rest at room temperature for 30 minutes before sheeting (see page 80).

2. Alternatively, you can let the dough rest for up to 24 hours in the refrigerator. The color sometimes darkens after that, although the dough is still usable for up to 3 days.

'NDUJA DOUGH

ORANGE

On paper, 'nduja is a spicy, spreadable pork paste. That description will either intrigue or off-put, depending on who you are. But gird your loins, my friends, because if you like a bit of well-balanced spiciness, one lick of this will stir you like a shih tzu in heat. Get ready to slather it on everything from grilled cheese to your lover's lips. Calabrian chile peppers and prosciutto tag team in this tube of temptation, and your defenses are no match for such a punchy, piquant pair. 'Nduja is readily available domestically at natural foods stores such as Whole Foods. La Quercia is a common brand.

3 tablespoons 'nduja
3 large eggs
1 tablespoon hot water
2 cups plus 2 tablespoons "00" pasta flour

1. In a blender, mix the 'nduja, eggs, and hot water on low speed to combine, slowly increasing speed until a smooth puree forms.

2. Combine the flour and puree in the bowl of a standing mixer fitted with a paddle attachment and mix on low speed until a ball of dough forms. Continue to knead for 3 minutes, either by hand or in the mixer, so that the dough develops elasticity and silkiness. Cover the ball of dough in plastic wrap and let it rest at room temperature for 30 minutes before sheeting (see page 80).

3. Alternatively, you can let the dough rest for up to 24 hours in the refrigerator. The color sometimes fades or intensifies after that, although the dough is still usable for up to 3 days.

HARISSA DOUGH
BRIGHT ORANGE

Harissa is a versatile, flavorful pepper spice paste with smoky, elegant notes. Good harissa bolsters the foods you choose to serve it with rather than overpowers them, as some hot sauces can. Trader Joe's sells a fire-hued harissa that has just enough heat. It is especially beloved in meat stews. Pasta made from this dough pairs well with ragù made with Spiced Lamb Yogurt Sauce (page 246). I use this dough when I'm after a truly orange color.

3 tablespoons harissa
3 large eggs
2¼ cups "OO" pasta flour

1. In a blender, mix the harissa and eggs on low speed to combine, slowly increasing speed until a smooth puree forms.

2. Combine the flour and puree in the bowl of a standing mixer fitted with a paddle attachment and mix on low speed until a ball of dough forms. Continue to knead for 3 minutes, either by hand or in the mixer, so that the dough develops elasticity and silkiness. Cover the ball of dough in plastic wrap and let it rest at room temperature for 30 minutes before sheeting (see page 80).

3. Alternatively, you can let the dough rest for up to 24 hours in the refrigerator. The color sometimes intensifies after that, although the dough is still usable for up to 3 days.

PAPRIKA DOUGH
ORANGE

Paprika is my stranded-on-a-desert-island spice. I love it Spanish or Hungarian, sweet, hot, mild, or smoky. You name it and I probably have it in my shamefully bloated paprika collection. Because there are so many different paprikas out there, purchase carefully if color is a big factor in you making paprika pasta. If you buy from the bulk section you can see the exact shade of paprika you're getting, and that will translate to the finished look of the noodles.

1 tablespoon paprika of your choice, based on the color you're after
4 large eggs
2¼ cups "00" pasta flour

1. In a blender, mix the paprika and eggs on low speed to combine, slowly increasing speed until a smooth puree forms.

2. Combine the flour and puree in the bowl of a standing mixer fitted with a paddle attachment and mix on low speed until a ball of dough forms. Continue to knead for 3 minutes, either by hand or in the mixer, so that the dough develops elasticity and silkiness. Cover the ball of dough in plastic wrap and let it rest at room temperature for 30 minutes before sheeting (see page 80).

3. Alternatively, you can let the dough rest for up to 24 hours in the refrigerator. The color sometimes darkens after that, although the dough is still usable for up to 3 days.

BEET-PAPRIKA DOUGH
BRIGHT RED

This is the dough to make if you are going for a bright red color. If you're aiming for orange-red, add an additional teaspoon of paprika. Not all paprika is created equal. When I select paprika with pasta dough in mind, I like to choose a bright, sweet version rather than one that is smoky and rust-colored. Most bulk spice counters will have at least a couple of choices of paprika in larger jars that make it easy to see the color inside. As with the red beet dough, if color is your primary motivating factor for making this dough, consider using frozen beets. Since more of the water content is removed from the beet upon freezing, it yields a very consistently vibrant color.

1 small beet (about 2 ounces), peeled and chopped (or use 2 ounces frozen beet chunks; see page 21)
4 teaspoons paprika
3 large eggs
2¼ cups flour

1. Put the beet in a small, non-metal bowl and cover with plastic wrap. Microwave for 50 seconds. Let sit for 2 minutes. Uncover and add to a blender along with the paprika and eggs. Blend on low speed to combine, slowly increasing speed until a smooth puree forms.

2. Combine the flour and puree in the bowl of a standing mixer fitted with a paddle attachment and mix on low speed until a ball of dough forms. Continue to knead for 3 minutes, either by hand or in the mixer, so that the dough develops elasticity and silkiness. Cover the ball of dough in plastic wrap and let it rest at room temperature for 30 minutes before sheeting (see page 80).

3. Alternatively, you can let the dough rest for up to 24 hours in the refrigerator. The dough will turn reddish brown after that, although the dough is still usable for up to 3 days.

EVERYTHING YOU NEED TO KNOW ABOUT COOKING YOUR STUNNING NOODLES

Rather than repeat cooking instructions for pasta on every single page, I'm providing this handy reference guide. In certain recipes where the pasta must be cooked in a particular fashion (cold noodles for dipping sauce and egg yolk ravioloni come to mind), I indicate the specific steps. A careful read of this section will give you the skills, knowledge, and confidence to consistently cook noodles the way you like them, every time.

Cooking pasta is a method (dare I say a philosophy?), not a recipe, and you need to be familiar and comfortable with how to approach it so you can adjust it to accommodate varying factors such as thickness of the noodle, type of sauce you're serving it with, and even how much pasta you are cooking at once.

TIMING THE SAUCE AND EXTRAS AROUND YOUR PASTA

Fresh pasta cooks fast, and most sauces do not, in comparison. For this reason your sauce should be nearly finished before your pasta so much as dips her toe in the boiling bath. Make sure you've taken your sauce as far as you need to before you boil the pasta, as there is nothing worse than removing pasta from the pasta water only to have it sit and congeal in a colander.

Along with the sauce, make sure everything you intend to serve with the pasta is ready to go. This would include extra cheese to be grated on top, fresh herbs, and mix-ins such as olives, mozzarella balls, lemon zest, fresh vegetables, and so on.

As they do in Italy, I love to serve pasta as a course unto itself, because then guests give it the full attention it deserves. I'm a purist in the sense that if a meal includes pasta, nothing else is on my plate at that time. Salad can wait and appetizers should have already been consumed. If a meat course is in the cards, side vegetables can happily sidle in beside it. It's probably freakish that I can gaze lovingly into a plate of pasta's "eyes," but I can and do, and I encourage any dinner guests to do the same, preferably over a bottle of nice Nebbiolo.

There's a second, secretly practical reason for pasta to exist as its own course, and that's so that you're not so busy pulling sides from the oven and salads from the fridge that your pasta goes cold and gummy. I won't fault you for choosing what works in your house, but if you do decide to serve pasta among other dishes, make sure they're all ready and waiting at the table before you cook the noodles. Look around. Is the salad dressing out? Does everyone have what they need to drink already at the table? If it's a dinner party, do the guests know they'll be expected to take a seat in a matter of moments?

For me, at least, pasta is the priority, and when I put so much of my heart into it, I want people to enjoy it passionately. Spending a few extra minutes getting everything and everyone ready before the pasta hits the water will limit the stress and anxiety surrounding the chaos of finishing multiple dishes at once.

This is as good a place as any to point out that guests model their hosts during parties. If you're organized, cool, calm, and collected, it will be that much easier to keep a smile on your face, and subsequently the faces of your lovely guests. Do as much as you can before they arrive (even if *they* are just your family rolling in to the kitchen from the living room), and dinner will come off beautifully.

TO STRAIN OR TO DRAIN: CHOOSING YOUR INSTRUMENTS OF TORTURE

The first thing you'll need is a pot filled with plenty of water for the amount of noodles you wish to cook. Individually, the batches of pasta dough in this book will cook well in a 6-quart stockpot, but if you're doubling the recipes, consider boiling in batches or using an 8-quart or larger stockpot.

If you're cooking gnocchi or ravioli, remove the pasta from the water using a spider, large slotted spoon, or other form of handheld strainer.

If you're cooking in batches, it's useful to remove the pasta from the water using a handheld instrument, as you won't want to pour out all of your water only to boil new water. A pasta insert, sometimes called a strainer insert, is one way to overcome this problem, but a handheld strainer will also be fine if you don't wish to invest in an insert.

I am infatuated with tools with perforations in them, and have just about every slotted spoon, spoodle, scoop colander, and fine-mesh strainer ever made. I'm always reaching to different tools for different pasta extraction needs, but if I had to choose just one, it would be the stainless-steel skimmer by Eastman Outdoors.

BOILING, *SALTED*, STARCHY WATER

Close your eyes, open your mouth just a tad, and imagine that a mermaid has placed her breast just within reach of your tongue. Give it a healthy lick—boy, girl, gay, straight, don't tell me you wouldn't slurp a mermaid if you had the chance—and now open your eyes and salt your water to taste just like the puckery protuberance of that mythical maiden. I mean, I could have said salty like the sea, but something tells me you'll remember this rule of breast best.

Lucky for you, I've done the salient saline calculations, and 1 tablespoon kosher salt for every quart of water will do the trick. I use Diamond Crystal kosher salt for everything except finishing dishes, as do most restaurant chefs. If you enter a restaurant and see Morton's salt, well, I won't exactly say run, but it's not the best sign. Chefs prefer Diamond Crystal for its crystal structure, its weight (Diamond weighs 5 ounces per cup versus Morton's 8 ounces per cup), and the fact that it doesn't contain the anti-caking agent ferrocyanide, as Morton's does. Unless otherwise specified, whenever I call for salt in this book, I am referring to Diamond Crystal.

And since we are on the subject of salts, I have three favorite finishing salts that you would use if you wanted to add a hint of salt to a prepared dish of pasta without adding Parmigiano-Reggiano (did you know Italians use this as a finishing cheese to add a bit of saltiness to pasta?). So if you're eliminating cheese for whatever reason but you want to check that same satisfying sprinkling box off your pretty plated pasta, I suggest Maldon, Murray River, or Cyprus Black Lava salt. The first is white, the second pink, and the final one black. It's nice to have all of them on hand and choose which to use based on what color crystal specks go best with your dish. It's also fun to blind taste all three and note the flavor and textural differences.

WHEN SHOULD I SALT THE WATER?

Some say it can pit the pan if you add salt before the water is boiling, depending on cookware and heat source (gas, induction, electric). Using induction and steel pans, I haven't had that issue, but if you're concerned, wait until the water is boiling to add the salt. The most important thing is that you actually add the salt, however, so if you're the forgetful type, add it early so it doesn't slip your mind while you're busy with other things, like stirring sauce or wrangling guests.

SEMOLINA STARCHINESS

The reason for calling for pasta water in any sauce is because it's flavored and thickened by the pasta, which adds character and body to the final sauce. Unless you're cooking batch after batch of pasta, in which case your pasta water will be plenty thick, toss a handful of semolina flour into the boiling, salted water to give the water enough starchiness to emulsify the final sauce. I suggest using semolina because it's granular enough that it won't clump together the way other flours might, but if you don't have it, you can quickly whisk in plain flour, taking care to scatter it into the water rather than dump it.

Use 1 tablespoon semolina for every quart of water, and note that this is only necessary if you're making sauce that calls for pasta water.

HOW LONG SHOULD I BOIL MY PASTA?

Generally speaking, you should cook your pasta al dente, or just to the point that the outside is soft, but the inside still has some bite. This guideline can be tailored to your specific taste if you wish for a mushier or firmer texture. The best way—whenever possible—to tell if your pasta is cooked properly is to remove a small piece of it from the boiling water and bite into it.

The thickness, age, temperature, and storage of pasta all impact the cooking time. And that's just fresh pasta I'm talking about. If it's thin, fresh off the rollers, and has merely rested at room temperature for 30 minutes, it's likely that it will cook in less than a minute. If it's thicker, it may take 2 minutes. If you pulled it from the fridge after a longer rest, add a minute to the cooking time—but test, test, test.

Finally, consider the sauce you're serving the pasta with. If the pasta hits the sauce and cooks a bit longer in it before service, undercook it by a minute so that it doesn't get soggy in the sauce. Never cook the pasta in the sauce for more than a few minutes unless you're deliberately aiming for a limp-textured noodle.

BASIC PASTA SHEETING TECHNIQUES

WHAT YOU'LL NEED

THE MEANS TO ROLL AND SHEET PASTA DOUGH

This can be as basic as a rolling pin or as complex as a pasta sheeting machine, which can be hand-cranked or motor-operated. Popular models include the Atlas Marcato (there's a manual and electric version), or a mixer attachment such as the KitchenAid or Kenwood. The Atlas Marcatos are my favorite small-batch pasta machines because they function perfectly, motor- or hand- cranked, come in a variety of fun colors, and are made extremely well.

If you want to go bigger, consider the Imperia Electric B220 model available in the United States through Emilio Miti. It has the advantage of a faster motor, which pushes dough through quickly, and has a wider roller base of 8¼ inches, as opposed to the mixer attachment models, which are between 5 and 6 inches. I use both the Imperia Electric and the motorized Atlas Marcato. If you're not sure where to invest, you can always start with the hand-cranked Atlas Marcato, and if your obsession grows, know that you can add a motor to it later without having to buy a whole new machine body.

CLEAN KITCHEN TOWELS

I like to purchase dedicated kitchen towels that will only ever be used to cover pasta. Once they are full of flour and gloppy from stray splashes of filling, I wash them and turn them into kitchen towels I use for other things. I like to use brand-new ones because they don't have any lint from the dryer or odd bits sticking to them, whereas older kitchen towels are less pristine and can leave unwanted debris on your pasta. Turns out this is a good system, as it helps me cycle through towels at about the time they all need replacing.

I like the very plainest, softest kitchen towels, like flour sack material, and I prefer plain white, so if I am lightly spraying them with water to keep the pasta underneath hydrated, I can tell that the water is absorbing uniformly. A painted-on pattern might prevent water transference in some areas. Is that anal? Yes, yes, it is.

WORK SURFACE

Any countertop surface will work for sheeting pasta, although wood is the best. It's easiest to cut pasta against wood; smooth stone surfaces will sometimes result in tears in the pasta as it flops around on the stone. The surface should be at least three feet wide, the bigger the better. If your countertop is tiled, you'll want to invest in a wooden cutting board or tabletop surface. I like to scour places like HomeGoods or Ross stores and buy the biggest cutting boards I can find. I have a collection of them, but storage doesn't get too out of hand as they perch very well vertically in the garage. IKEA also has some inexpensive wood surfaces in the kitchen section.

BENCH SCRAPER

I defined this earlier on page 16, and look: It's already coming in handy.

DOUGH

A ball of dough (the recipes start on page 39). If you've never made pasta before, start with the basic dough and master it, as it's easy to work with and shape and gives you a real sense of what pasta should feel like in your hands.

WHAT TO KNOW BEFORE YOU START

BATCHES

Many of the sheeted pasta recipes in this book call for amounts of dough that are less than a full batch. I find it easiest to make dough in whole batches and then portion off the amount of dough you need to make a specific recipe. Trying to make less than a whole batch of dough is often tricky if there isn't enough material in a blender, mixer, or food processor for it to function properly. Conversely, trying

to triple and quadruple batches of dough can overtax your equipment and cause motors to burn out before they've lived their natural lives.

The end result of making whole batches when you need only a quarter or even a sixth of that dough is that you'll have plenty of leftover pasta dough in the refrigerator. I see this as an opportunity, rather than a problem. If you haven't used it for something specific after three days, consider sheeting it into an easy-to-make noodle that you can dry for later use.

UNDERSTANDING HUMIDITY AND TEMPERATURE

One of the reasons I like to make pasta everywhere I travel is because I find it interesting to test how my standard dough does in different weather conditions. Humidity and temperature play a big part in this. If it's hot and sticky outside, your pasta is going to be wetter and soggier than if it's dry and cold. Air-conditioning, rain, wind, and all manner of weather play a part in your pasta, but the good news is everything is correctable. If the dough feels sticky, add a little bit more flour. If it feels too dry, keep it covered as much as possible and use a clean water spraying bottle to finely mist the dough as you're sheeting it. Good pasta is flexible. You should be too.

HANDLING DOUGH WITH CARE

Long fingernails are the enemy of pasta sheets. I suggest a tidy trim if you don't want to puncture your hard-won works of pasta art. When you're passing pasta sheets through the pasta rolling machine, get comfortable with using the backs and palms of your hands more than your fingertips, so that you can minimize potential punctures. If you've chosen to work with a large batch of dough at one time, be sure to support the dough as it comes out of the rolling machine by draping it over your arms and letting the counter bear some of the weight.

LAMINATING DOUGH

By folding the dough back on itself several times, you ensure that the resulting pasta sheet will be tensile and pliant. Lamination develops strength in the sheet so that when you manipulate it into different shapes and color combinations, it's supple and does not fray and crack.

Another benefit of laminating dough is that if (due to machine error, never human; I'm giving you the benefit of the doubt here) you wind up with a pasta sheet that is inconsistent or has jagged edges, you can tri-fold it on itself like a letter, then re-sheet it. This smooths out irregularities.

How can you tell if dough has been laminated enough? It will go from feeling

rough, gummy, or tensile to feeling elastic and smooth. I generally laminate five times. I understand that hand-cranking a pasta roller is tedious, if that's the equipment you're using, so it will be our little secret if you want to laminate only twice.

SCRAPS

Don't throw out dough scraps after you've sheeted and shaped pasta. Instead, channel your inner *cucina povera*. Roll scraps into a ball and store in a zip-top bag to use in the garganelli recipe on page 132, re-sheet them into any pasta shape you see fit, or

make crackers (page 77). You don't have to keep pasta scrap colors segregated. Roll all the colors into one ball and see what kinds of random, tie-dye-esque patterns you get.

If you really don't think you'll reuse the scraps for whatever reason, you can still upcycle them. Boil them and toss them in a bit of butter, then give a bite to the nearest kid or kid-at-heart. (It's okay if this is you.) They'll love the funny-shaped, doughy bits of starchy color. As a last resort, feed scraps to backyard chickens or very lucky house pets.

CRACKERS

You can make very passable crackers out of pasta dough scraps. I find this comes in handy when I've spent the day pasta making and neglected to think about an appetizer for when guests arrive. Serving homemade crackers with a wedge of cheese, spread, olives, fruit, or any old creamy thing you find in the back of the fridge makes it look as if you devoted hours to antipasti, not minutes.

Sheet dough to the third level of thinness on a pasta machine and cut it into cracker-size pieces using a straight or fluted rolling cutter. I prefer cutting them to saltine size, because it's just right for scooping. Poke each cracker with fork tines a few times to prevent too many air pockets from forming while baking. Have fun with your poking—you can stab at random or create a pattern of holes as on commercial crackers.

Top the crackers with a brush of olive oil and a smattering of finishing salt, then bake on a sheet pan in a preheated 450°F oven until lightly browned and crisp, 5 to 7 minutes. Watch the crackers carefully as they're baking, because depending on the thinness they can brown very quickly. Cool the crackers on a wire rack, where they'll become even crisper. When they're completely cool you can store them in an airtight container for up to 5 days.

PASTINA

Many of the pasta pattern techniques you'll learn in the coming pages require you to repeatedly punch out the same shape using a plunger cutter. These pasta shapes—little stars, hearts, or dots, for example—are very pretty on their own but serve no further purpose in the making of the pattern. Rather than scrap them, I save all of my little shapes, called pastina, or "tiny pasta," in Italian. Because they don't have much surface area, they dry very well without cracking, unlike larger pasta. I let them dry fully, then store them in an open jar, because an airtight container encourages mold growth. When I have a few handfuls, I toss them into thin, brothy soups, or even just store-bought chicken stock if I'm in a pinch. Colorful *pastina in brodo* is the ultimate sick-kid comfort food, because in addition to being easily digestible, it's also fun to eat.

STORING, FREEZING, AND DRYING PASTA

I rarely freeze pasta, with the exception of gnocchi and unsheeted pasta dough, which both freeze well. Freeze gnocchi in a single layer, then store in an airtight freezer bag. Store unsheeted pasta dough in a freezer bag or sealed Foodsaver bag. Both keep well for two weeks, possibly even a month if well-stored in a temperature-consistent freezer.

While you can freeze sheeted pasta, it dries and cracks in the freezer within a couple of weeks, so it doesn't seem worth it. There's also usually a higher moisture content in colored pasta because of the added tint ingredient and because I designed the dough to be more malleable so that you can easily shape it into designs and patterns. This means that noodles made from it will fracture more frequently than store-bought or stiffer homemade pasta would.

The bottom line is that you'll want to serve the pasta projects in this book when they're at the peak of their beauty. There are some refrigerator resting and holding options in case you want to plan a meal a couple of days in advance. One thing to note is not to cover filled pasta such as agnolotti or caramelle when it is in the refrigerator or the filling will leech into the pasta, making it soggy.

On the rare occasions I don't use all the noodles I have sheeted and cut, I prefer to dry them on a sheet pan on the counter and use them much the way I would dried noodles from a box. I store dried noodles in a paper bag and use them within a week, to avoid excessive breakage.

SHEETING PASTA, STEP BY STEP

1. Divide the dough in half and work with one half at a time. Cover the dough you aren't using in plastic wrap so that it doesn't dry out. Sheet the first half following the next steps and repeat with the remaining dough half once the first half is at the desired thinness.

2. After you've made pasta several times and working with half a ball of dough is easy peasy, go ahead and tackle the whole batch of dough at once if you wish. You'll get a better rolling pin workout this way.

3. Using a rolling pin, roll the dough into a rough rectangle, about ¼ inch thick and no wider than the rollers on your pasta machine. Dust with flour as needed so that the dough doesn't stick to the pin or work surface.

4. Set the roller on the pasta machine to the widest setting. Be sure to look at the rollers to confirm you're at the widest setting, as the markings on different machines count either in ascending or descending order, from 1 on up or from 6 to 9 on down.

5. Feed the pasta dough through the rollers on the widest setting. Feed it through again on the second-widest setting. Fold the dough in half lengthwise and flour both sides.

6. Feed the sheet through on the widest setting again, then feed it through on the third-widest setting. Fold it in thirds, like a letter destined for an envelope. (Never fold the dough wider than the rollers or the dough will not pass through easily and will tear. But if the dough does tear, never fear. Just sandwich two torn pieces together and re-roll them. The pasta sheet will come together beautifully and no one will ever be the wiser.)

7. Flour both sides of the pasta sheet. Feed the dough through on the widest setting, then the third-widest setting. Repeat the folding and feeding steps two more times to develop strength and elasticity in the dough (see "Laminating Dough," page 72), flouring as needed.

8. Now you're ready to roll the dough to the desired level of thinness. I tend never to use sheets thicker than the fourth-thinnest setting, and for very delicate noodles such as tajarin or angel hair, I roll the dough to the thinnest setting my pasta dough will allow without feeling as if it's going to tear. In each recipe I give suggestions for how thin to sheet your pasta, but there's flexibility within those parameters depending on the final texture you want. If you're having trouble deciding how thin to roll your noodles, consider the sauce. Noodles that will be served with light, stock-based sauces or just a coating of oil or butter fare very well made extra thin. On the other hand, a thick ragù or sugo needs noodles with some girth, so don't go too thin.

9. After the pasta is sheeted to the desired thinness, cover it with a clean kitchen towel and let it rest for a few minutes, then proceed with the recipe.

SOMETHING FUN: Make three batches of noodles, each a different thickness. Boil them all and do a taste test. Al dente lovers often like thicker noodles because they're harder to overcook, but the gem worth gleaning from this experiment is that pasta is subjective. I want to set you up with all the tools to make pasta *your* bitch, not mine, and to do that, you need to know how you like it.

FETTUCCINE

Fettuccine are amenable to a wide variety of sauces, which is probably why this is the most widely known (not to be confused with the widest, lol) of all the sheeted pasta noodles. You can go far in life if you're armed with the ability to make a batch of fettuccine from scratch. For example, you could ensnare a lover in its twisty tendrils, or broker a deal for world peace, if you can just get all the international leaders together for a meal of your magical noodles. Fact: People who are enamored of pasta are less petulant than their non-carby counterparts. Source: my own informal observations over plenty of plates of fettuccine. Wine helps too.   MAKES 4 SERVINGS

1 batch dough (your choice of color)
Flour for dusting
Kosher salt

1. Roll the dough to your desired level of thinness on a pasta machine. If you're a fettuccine-making virgin, stop at the second-thinnest setting on a pasta machine.

2. Using a straight rolling cutter, cut the pasta sheet into 12-inch lengths. Lightly flour each length and layer them on a floured surface with a kitchen towel between each layer and on the top of the stack. Let the sheets rest for 10 minutes.

3. Feed each pasta sheet through the fettuccine cutter on the pasta machine and hang to rest (see page 16). Let the fettuccine hang for 30 minutes, or until it feels leathery. Carefully remove it to a lightly floured sheet pan, forming it into little "nests" so that it's easy to pick up each one and plunge it into boiling water.

4. If you would like to cook it another day, store the pasta on the sheet pan covered with plastic wrap in the refrigerator for up to 3 days. Increase the cooking time by 1 minute if working with refrigerated pasta.

5. Boil in salted water for 2 minutes, drain, dress, and serve immediately.

PAPPARDELLE

Pappardelle is one of the easiest shapes of pasta to make, and a good "by hand" option to practice your rolling cutter skills, as you can easily make it without a pasta cutting machine attachment. The standard for cutting pappardelle is not exact, and I like to embrace the homemade look, so if each noodle is a few millimeters bigger than its neighbor, so be it. I tend to cut my pappardelle ¾ to 1 inch wide, and a good rule of thumb for length is 12 inches. It can be cut with either a fluted or a straight rolling cutter. A straight rolling cutter will produce less waste, but the fluted look is admittedly impressive. MAKES 4 SERVINGS

1 batch dough (your choice of color)
Flour for dusting
Kosher salt

1. Roll the dough to the second-thinnest setting on a pasta machine. Using a fluted or straight rolling cutter, cut the pasta sheet into 2-foot lengths. Lightly flour each length and layer them on a floured surface with a kitchen towel between each layer and on the top of the stack. Let the sheets rest for 15 minutes.

2. Working with one sheet at a time, cut lengthwise strips that are ¾ to 1 inch wide. Cut the strips in half to make pieces that are 12 inches long. Hang the noodles to rest (see page 16) and repeat the process with the remaining pasta sheets.

3. Let the pappardelle rest for 30 minutes or up to 2 hours at room temperature before boiling. If you would like to cook it another day, after it is leathery to the touch and no longer sticky, store the

pasta on a sheet pan covered with plastic wrap in the refrigerator for up to 3 days. Increase the cooking time by 1 minute if working with refrigerated pasta.

4. Boil in salted water for 2 minutes, drain, dress, and serve immediately.

LASAGNE SHEETS

This is the ideal shape to showcase large, ornate pasta patterns. When you've gone to all the trouble to lay out an argyle pattern with pasta, for example, it's almost painful to cut it into tiny noodles, so a large-format noodle starts looking mighty attractive. You can use these sheets in an actual lasagna, but you can also treat them like pappardelle (cut them to ¾ to 1 inch wide) and boil and toss them with your favorite sauce.

If you're making single-colored lasagne sheets and you intend to serve them in a baked lasagna, consider the size of your pan when you're sheeting and cutting. These instructions will give you enough pasta for one lasagna at four sheets per layer, laid crosswise in a 9 by 13-inch pan, but your needs may vary.

MAKES ENOUGH PASTA FOR A 9 BY 13-INCH LASAGNA, TO SERVE 8

1 batch dough (your choice of color)
Flour for dusting
Kosher salt (if pre-boiling)

1. Roll the dough to the second-thinnest setting on a pasta machine. Keep the pasta sheet as wide as your pasta rollers will allow, ideally 6 inches.

2. Using a fluted or straight rolling cutter, cut the pasta sheet into 2-foot lengths. Lightly flour each length and layer them on a floured surface with a kitchen towel between each layer and on the top of the stack. Let the sheets rest for 10 minutes.

3. Working with one sheet at a time, cut lengthwise strips about 3 inches wide. Cut the strips in thirds to make six pieces that are 3 by 8 inches.

4. Let the lasagne sheets rest for 30 minutes or up to 2 hours at room temperature before boiling. If you would

like to cook the pasta another day, after it's leathery to the touch and no longer sticky, store it on a sheet pan covered with plastic wrap in the refrigerator for up to 3 days.

5. If you're layering these sheets into an actual lasagna, pre-boiling the sheets is optional. The benefit of pre-boiling is that the pasta will absorb less moisture from the sauce, making for a saucier lasagna, but on the other hand the lasagne sheets won't stay as firm. It's a matter of textural preference. If you choose to pre-cook them, boil the sheets one at a time in salted water for 15 seconds and lay them flat on a drying rack to cool before layering them into lasagna.

HAND-CUT TAJARIN

Tajarin, pronounced " tie-yar-EEN," is Piemontese dialect for "tagliarini." It's a whisper-thin, hand-cut noodle that's deceptively difficult because the goal is to make them as thin and uniform as possible. Since they're so diminutive and lithe, they're best with the lightest kiss of sauce—think sage browned butter.

Classically, this shape is made with just flour and egg yolks rather than whole eggs or the vegetable-egg purees featured here. My recipe focuses more on the shape than the dough consistency, but yolk-intense tajarin die-hards are welcome to swap in 3 egg yolks for every 1 whole egg if they wish.   MAKES 4 SERVINGS

1 batch dough (your choice of color)
Flour for dusting
Kosher salt

1. Roll the dough to the thinnest setting on a pasta machine. Be sure to liberally flour the sheet of pasta, as you don't want it to stick together. Cut the pasta sheet into 12-inch lengths, let them rest for 5 minutes, flip them over, and let them rest 5 minutes more.

2. When the sheets are leathery to the touch but not yet brittle, they're ready to cut. Work with one length at a time. Flour one side of a sheet lightly and evenly on top. Gently roll the sheet into a loose tube as you would a poster.

3. Carefully press the tube down so that it will be thin enough to cut, but not so much that you risk it sticking to itself. Using either a bench scraper or a chef's knife, julienne the roll into pasta strips

as thin as you can make them—aim for 1⁄16 inch. Using both hands and all your fingers, "fluff" the cut pasta pieces so that they unfurl into long strands. Repeat with the remaining sheets of pasta.

4. Let the tajarin rest for 30 minutes or up to 2 hours at room temperature before boiling. If you would like to cook the pasta another day, after it's leathery to the touch and no longer sticky, store it on a sheet pan covered with plastic wrap in the refrigerator for up to 2 days. Increase the cooking time by 30 seconds if working with refrigerated pasta.

5. Boil in salted water for 1 minute, drain, dress, and serve immediately.

PASTA ALLA CHITARRA

One of my favorite ways to cut pasta is with a special gadget called a *chitarra*, which means "guitar" in Italian. It's a wooden instrument from Abruzzo with guitar-like strings running down both sides, one with strings that are 3 millimeters apart, which will produce pasta comparable to angel hair, and the other with strings 5 millimeters apart, which results in noodles more like fettuccine. To use a *chitarra*, you press a sheet of pasta through your chosen side. The texture of *chitarra* noodles is entirely different from that of their knife- or machine-cut counterparts because of the squared side edge the guitar string makes along the noodles.

When I'm making pasta with a *chitarra*, I like to start with pasta sheets on the thick side before pressing them through the strings, which results in noodles with four distinct sides rather than just a front and a back, but the thickness is entirely up to you—experiment to see what you like best.

You can easily source a pasta *chitarra* online for between $20 and $50, and since it's such a specialty item, most are still well constructed and made in Italy.

You can work with single-colored or two-sided dough on the *chitarra*. If you want bicolored noodles, just follow the recipe for two-toned fettuccine (page 96) but use these *chitarra*-cutting instructions, not the machine instructions given there.

MAKES 4 SERVINGS

SPECIAL EQUIPMENT
Chitarra

1 batch dough (your choice of color)
Flour for dusting
Kosher salt

1. Roll the dough to the fourth-thinnest setting on a pasta machine. Using a straight rolling cutter, cut the pasta sheet into 12-inch lengths. Do not be tempted to cut the sheets to the full length of the *chitarra* strings, as the sheets will stretch as you press them through and you need enough room to accommodate this stretching. Lightly flour each sheet and layer them on a floured surface with a kitchen towel between each layer and on the top of the stack. Let the sheets rest for 10 minutes.

2. Choose whether you are making 3 millimeter or 5 millimeter noodles and place that side of the *chitarra* facing up, with the strings perpendicular to the edge

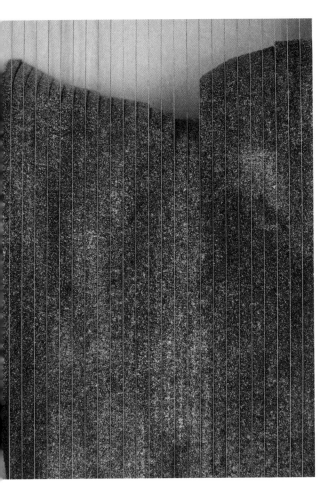

of your work surface. Center a pasta sheet along the length of the *chitarra* and use a rolling pin to press the sheet through the strings. At first you will roll in the standard motion of a rolling pin, but after the noodles are about halfway through the strings, stop rolling the pin and instead press it up and down the length of the strings, which will push the noodles all the way through. Once you can see all the metal strings through the sheet, use your

fingers to "strum" the noodles down off the strings, where they will fall onto the wooden surface below. Turn the *chitarra* on its side and the noodles will fall out into your waiting hand.

3. Hang the noodles to rest (see page 16). Repeat with the remaining sheets. Let the pasta hang for 15 minutes, or until it feels leathery to the touch. Carefully remove it to a lightly floured sheet pan, forming it

into little "nests" so that it's easy to pick up each nest and plunge it into boiling water.

4. If you would like to cook it another day, store the pasta on the sheet pan covered with plastic wrap in the refrigerator for up to 3 days. Increase the cooking time by 1 minute if working with refrigerated pasta.

5. Boil in salted water for 2 minutes, drain, dress, and serve immediately.

NOTE: *If the strings on your chitarra feel loose, you can tighten them by slowly turning the bolts on the side of the device using a flathead screwdriver or the blunt edge of a butter knife. Be careful not to tighten the strings too much or you can snap them, just as on a regular guitar. It is a good idea to store the chitarra with the bolts backed off a quarter turn so that constant tension doesn't prematurely wear it out.*

COLORFUL FARFALLE

Farfalle, or "butterflies," are fun, easy, and extremely versatile as far as pasta shapes go. Once you've mastered making several different flavors of dough, farfalle are good noodles to make to showcase them. The following technique demonstrates how to shape farfalle and calls for one batch of dough. If you would like to make several colors, just pinch off pieces from each of the different dough colors until you have approximately the amount of one batch of dough for four servings of pasta.

MAKES 4 SERVINGS

1 batch dough (your choice of color) or the equivalent of 1 batch dough, composed of two or more different colors
Flour for dusting
Kosher salt

1. Roll the dough (keeping colors separate if you're using more than one) to the second-thinnest setting on a pasta machine. Farfalle are a flexible shape, and if you wish to roll them to the thinnest setting to make extra-delicate little butterflies, that's fine too; just don't pinch them too hard when shaping and don't overcook them, as they will tear if you're too rough. If you use multiple colors, roll each separately through the machine.

2. Work with 2 feet of lightly floured pasta sheet at a time, with the rest covered under a kitchen towel to ensure it doesn't dry out. Using a rolling cutter, cut the sheet into rectangles that are about 1½ by 2 inches. (I like to cut the long sides of the farfalle with a straight rolling cutter and the short sides of the rectangle with a fluted cutter, to more

closely resemble butterfly wings. But if I'm trying to play up the bow tie rather than butterfly angle, I use a straight rolling cutter for all the cuts.)

3. Position the rectangles so that the long edges face you.

4. SHAPING OPTION 1: Place your thumb and forefinger on the bottom middle edge and direct middle of the farfalla and slide your thumb up toward your forefinger to make the first pinch, as shown on page 94. Now lift your forefinger to the top middle edge of the rectangle and pull the top toward your thumb so that the resulting farfalla is pleated and pinched in the middle.

SHAPING OPTION 2: Place your forefinger on the direct middle, your thumb on the bottom middle edge, and your middle

finger on the top middle edge of the farfalla. Bring your middle finger and thumb inward toward your forefinger in one pinching motion and release when the farfalla is pleated and pinched in the middle.

5. Let the farfalle rest for 30 minutes or up to 2 hours at room temperature before boiling. If you would like to cook

them another day, after they are leathery to the touch and no longer sticky, store the pasta on a sheet pan covered with plastic wrap in the refrigerator for up to 3 days. Increase the cooking time by 1 minute if working with refrigerated pasta.

6. Boil in salted water for 1 to 2 minutes, drain, dress, and serve immediately.

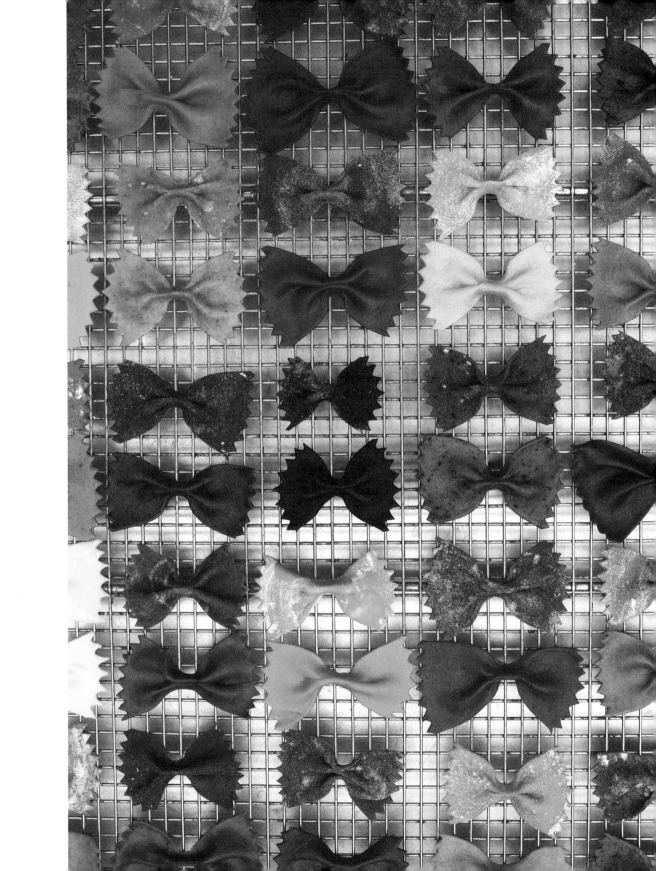

TWO-TONED FETTUCCINE

While one jolt of color is good, two is even better. This two-toned fettuccine is your first step toward total world domination through colored pasta. When you look back through the dough chapter, to decide which two doughs to press together, consider how they'll look together. Some of you will want to choose colors in celebration of your favorite football team, while others may be so obsessed with complementary colors that it's red-green, purple-yellow, or blue-orange all the way. If you want to re-create *paglia e fieno* fettuccine, use Basic Mother Dough (page 55) and Leafy Greens Dough (page 51).

Another thing you might keep in mind is backing a "stronger" dough with a weaker dough. Simply put, the doughs with more eggs in them will be stronger, meaning that they will tear less and be less droopy, whereas the doughs that are more water-based will stretch, sag, and tear if you aren't careful. Whenever I know I'm going to do a very detailed pasta project (such as one of those in the advanced sheeting chapter), I try to use Basic Mother Dough (page 55) as my "backing" so that any color I layer upon it will have a stable base, since it is the strongest of all the doughs in this book.

Finally, you might consider how you wish to serve the pasta when deciding which flavors to unite. If you're making Cold Noodle Dipping Sauce (page 224), buckwheat and matcha make a lovely flavor complement. Amp up a spicier sauce even more with harissa and 'nduja noodles, or conversely dial it back with something fresh and light, such as a combo of parsley-pepper-turmeric and carrot. MAKES 4 SERVINGS

½ batch dough (your choice of color)
½ batch dough (your choice of color)
Flour for dusting
Kosher salt

1. Roll each ½ batch of dough to the middle thinness on a pasta machine. (I like to roll each color through a particular machine setting rather than fully sheet one and then the other. It's ultimately less work switching back and forth between pieces of dough than adjusting the pasta machine several times.)

2. Flour a work surface and place one sheet of pasta upon it. If it feels a little dry, you can use a paper towel or pastry brush to dab it with a little water so that the top sheet of pasta will adhere to it. Gently place the second sheet of pasta over the first and use a rolling pin to lightly roll them together lengthwise, to

ensure that they won't flop apart. Reset the pasta machine to the thickest setting and roll the combined sheet through. Continue rolling down to your desired level of thinness. You may have to cut the pasta sheet in half if it gets too long to handle.

3. Using a straight rolling cutter, cut the pasta sheet into 12-inch lengths. Lightly flour each length and layer them on a floured surface with a kitchen towel between each layer and on the top of the stack. Let the sheets rest for 10 minutes.

4. Feed each pasta sheet through the fettuccine cutter on the pasta machine

and hang the fettucine to rest (see page 16) for 30 minutes, or until it feels leathery to the touch. Carefully remove it to a lightly floured sheet pan, forming it into little "nests" so that it's easy to pick up each one and plunge it into boiling water.

5. If you would like to cook it another day, store the pasta on the sheet pan covered with plastic wrap in the refrigerator for up to 3 days. Increase the cooking time by 1 minute if working with refrigerated pasta.

6. Boil in salted water for 2 minutes, drain, dress, and serve immediately.

SIX-COLORED FETTUCCINE

Here you'll learn how to make stripes with six colors on a pasta sheet. You can cut that into whatever final shape you want—pappardelle, lasagne, what have you—but I'll show it here as fettuccine and trust you to make your own shaping decisions in the end.

Don't work with too much dough at a time, or it will dry out and you'll get frustrated trying to (wo)manhandle a big ol' hunk of rainbow goo.   MAKES 4 SERVINGS

⅓ batch Basic Mother Dough (page 55)
Golf ball–size pieces of 6 different pasta dough flavors. For a classic
    rainbow, I suggest using Beet-Blueberry (page 40), Spirulina
    (page 44), Leafy Greens (page 51), Turmeric (page 56), Harissa
    (page 61), and Beet-Paprika (page 63).
Flour for dusting
Kosher salt

1. Sheet the basic pasta dough to the middle setting on a pasta machine, taking care to keep it as rectangular as possible with edges that go all the way to the sides of the pasta roller. Cover this sheet with a very lightly water-dampened kitchen towel in a place out of the way of the pasta machine.

2. Sheet the 6 dough flavors until they are the same length as the basic pasta sheet (the machine setting may vary, and that's okay). Dust them with flour, then run them through the fettuccine attachment on a pasta machine. Make each color into a little separate pile next to the basic pasta sheet. Wipe the basic pasta sheet with a damp paper towel so the "stripes" will adhere to it. Keep the paper towel handy in case you have to re-moisten partway through.

3. Working with one color strip at a time, lay it lengthwise along the basic pasta sheet, starting at one lengthwise edge. You can follow a color pattern from red to purple and repeat if you're going for the rainbow look, or use your imagination and create stripes in your own fun pattern. When the entire sheet of basic pasta dough is covered in stripes, lightly roll it with a rolling pin to make sure everything stays in place.

4. Cut the sheet into 5-inch lengths, or as long as the width of your pasta machine rollers, and re-roll them through a pasta machine to the desired thickness setting. Take care that you are rolling the sheet through horizontally now, with the stripes parallel to the roller. This is to ensure that each piece of pasta will have all of the colors on it, rather than the one or

FROM TOP TO BOTTOM:
Beet-Blueberry, Spirulina, Leafy Greens,
Turmeric, Harissa, and Beet-Paprika

two that it would have if you sheeted it lengthwise.

5. Lightly flour each sheet and layer them on a floured surface with a kitchen towel between each layer and on the top of the stack. Let the sheets rest for 10 minutes.

6. Feed each pasta sheet through the fettuccine cutter on a pasta machine and hang the noodles to rest (see page 16). Let the fettuccine hang for 30 minutes, or until it feels leathery to the touch. Carefully remove it to a lightly floured

sheet pan, forming it into little "nests" so that it's easy to pick up each one and plunge it into boiling water.

7. If you would like to cook it another day, store the pasta on the sheet pan covered in plastic wrap in the refrigerator for up to 3 days. Increase the cooking time by 1 minute if working with refrigerated pasta.

8. Boil in salted water for 2 minutes, drain, dress, and serve immediately.

FLUTE-PATTERNED PAPPARDELLE

I like to think of a fluted pattern on pappardelle noodles as fashionable food. They have a very Missoni-esque vibe, and the good news is that they are not very tricky to master, but they pack a pretty punch in the department of good looks. You can cut the patterned sheet this technique demonstrates into fettuccine or even lasagne noodles instead of pappardelle if you wish, but I find that pappardelle are just wide enough to make the pattern shine.

When you're deciding which three dough flavors to use, consider how harmonious the colors are together. The two colors that make the overlaid strips will pop brightly if the base color is lighter, but I've also had success using charcoal/black as a base dough and overlaying bright colors. Bold colors emanate a jewel-like quality when they're superimposed on a dark backing. MAKES 4 SERVINGS

½ batch dough (your choice of color; this is the base color)
Flour for dusting
¼ batch dough (your choice of color)
¼ batch dough (your choice of color)
Kosher salt

1. Roll the ½ batch of dough to the third-thinnest setting on a pasta machine. Lightly dust a work surface with flour and lay the base sheet over it, covered with a kitchen towel. Roll each ¼ batch of dough to the fourth-thinnest setting, taking care that each is the same width as the already-rolled base sheet.

2. Using a fluted pasta cutter, cut ½-inch-wide crosswise strips of each of the ¼-batch sheets of pasta. Uncover the base sheet and lightly moisten it with a damp paper towel so that the strips of colored dough will adhere to it. Alternating between the two colors, lay the strips one by one across the base sheet, leaving ¼-inch gaps of base color between them. You may not use all of the strips; any extra can be re-rolled for other uses.

3. Once you've covered the base sheet with colored strips, press a rolling pin along it to make sure all the strips are in place. Re-roll the now-flute-striped sheet of pasta, starting on the thickest setting and descending to the second-thinnest setting.

4. Using a fluted or straight rolling cutter, cut the pasta sheet into 2-foot lengths.

Lightly flour each length and layer them on a floured surface with a kitchen towel between each layer and on the top of the stack. Let the sheets rest for 10 minutes.

5. Working with one sheet at a time, cut lengthwise strips ¾ to 1 inch wide. Cut the strips in half to make pieces that are 12 inches long. Hang the noodles to rest (see page 16) and repeat the process with the remaining sheets.

6. Let the pappardelle rest for 30 minutes or up to 2 hours at room temperature before boiling. If you would like to cook the pasta another day, after it is leathery to the touch and no longer sticky, store it on a sheet pan covered with plastic wrap in the refrigerator for up to 3 days. Increase the cooking time by 1 minute if working with refrigerated pasta.

7. Boil in salted water for 2 minutes, drain, dress, and serve immediately.

DRAWING ON PASTA WITH PASTA

This is a delightful experiment in embracing the beauty of randomness. I love to do this when I have leftover pieces of several colors of dough, as it is an inventive way to reuse scraps. Keep in mind that some colors will show up better against other colors, so play around and see what works well together. When in doubt, use Basic Mother Dough (page 55) as your base sheet, as it's a very strong dough and most every color will pop against it.

This technique describes cutting the resulting pasta into lasagne strips, but you can turn it into whichever shape you wish, bearing in mind that larger shapes like pappardelle or ravioli will showcase the pattern well.

MAKES ENOUGH PASTA FOR AN 8 BY 13-INCH LASAGNA (8 SERVINGS)

½ batch pasta dough (your choice, basic works well)
Golf ball–size pieces or scraps of as many different pasta dough
    flavors as you'd like to use
Flour for dusting
Kosher salt (if pre-boiling)

1. Sheet the ½ batch of pasta dough to the middle setting on a pasta machine, taking care to keep it as rectangular and uniform as possible. Cover this base sheet with a very lightly water-dampened kitchen towel in a place out of the way of the pasta machine.

2. Sheet the additional pasta pieces to the second-thinnest setting on a pasta machine. Dust them with flour and run them through the spaghetti attachment of the pasta machine.

3. Uncover the base sheet and wipe it with a damp paper towel so the strands of spaghetti will adhere to it. Drop

individual strands, or even clumps, of spaghetti onto the base sheet until you have used all of them. Play with dropping them in sweeping, plunging, and flinging motions to experiment with different visual effects.

4. Once you have used all of the spaghetti strands, lightly roll the sheet with a pin to make sure everything stays in place.

5. Roll the sheet from the thickest to the second-thinnest setting on a pasta machine. Using a fluted or straight rolling cutter, cut the pasta sheet into 2-inch lengths. Lightly flour each length and

layer them on a floured surface with a kitchen towel between each layer and on the top of the stack. Allow the sheets to rest for 15 minutes.

6. Working with one sheet at a time, cut lengthwise strips 3 inches wide. Cut the strips into thirds to make pieces that measure 3 by 8 inches.

7. Allow the lasagne sheets to rest for 30 minutes or up to 2 hours at room temperature before boiling. If you would like to cook them another day, after they are leathery to the touch and no longer sticky, store the pasta on a sheet pan covered in plastic wrap in the refrigerator for up to 3 days.

8. Boil each sheet in salted water for 15 seconds and let cool flat on a drying rack before layering into lasagna.

CAVATELLI

While cavatelli is technically a rolled shape rather than a sheeted one, I've kept it in the basic sheeting chapter because it's made with any one of the twenty-five master doughs, in contrast with a rolled dough such as the gnocchi or gnudi.

You'll need a gnocchi board, sometimes called a cavatelli board, to get the distinctive grooves that are a trademark of this shape. The good news is that one can be had for less than $10 at many kitchen stores or online. Alternatively, you can use a silicone sushi mat to make the grooves—also an economical and practical solution.

Cavatelli is one of the easier shapes to make without a machine, should you wish to enjoy a day of true *pasta fatta a mano*, or "pasta made by hand."

The grooved nature of cavatelli makes it a good candidate for thicker sauces, such as Golden Milk Ragù (page 236). MAKES 4 SERVINGS

SPECIAL EQUIPMENT
A silicone sushi mat or a gnocchi board

1 batch dough (your choice of color)
Flour (and semolina, if needed) for dusting
Kosher salt

1. Roll the batch of dough to the second-*thickest* setting on a pasta machine. Flour the underside of the sheet and set it on a work surface. Using a straight rolling cutter, cut the dough lengthwise into 1-inch-wide strips. Using a bench scraper or chef's knife, cut the strips crosswise into ¼-inch pieces.

2. TO SHAPE WITH A BENCH SCRAPER (PREFERRED): Use the cutting edge of the bench scraper to pull each piece of dough *toward yourself* across the sushi mat.

TO SHAPE WITH YOUR THUMB: Use the side of your thumb to roll each piece of dough *away from yourself* across the sushi mat.

3. In either case, apply enough pressure so that the dough curls around itself and grooves are formed but not so much pressure that the dough sticks to the mat. If your dough is repeatedly sticking to the mat, flour it.

4. Repeat the process with the remaining pieces of dough. Let the cavatelli rest for 30 minutes or up to 2 hours at room temperature before boiling. If you would like to cook the pasta another day, store it on a parchment-lined and semolina-dusted sheet pan covered with plastic wrap in the refrigerator for up to 3 days.

Increase the cooking time by 1 minute if working with refrigerated pasta.

5. Boil in salted water for 2 to 3 minutes or until floating. Drain, dress, and serve immediately.

3

ADVANCED PASTA SHEETING TECHNIQUES

Congratulations! If you've already made a few pasta creations from the previous chapter, you're ready to graduate to something more complicated. The recipes and techniques in this chapter are a lot like the last, except you might have to juggle a few more pieces of dough and use an extra tool or two. I have complete confidence in your ability to tackle this chapter, so let's get started, pasta party people.

RAINBOW CAVATELLI

Please see the header in the Cavatelli recipe on page 108 for information on cavatelli boards, or what you can use in place of one to execute rainbow cavatelli.

This recipe got me in a lot of trouble across the Internet. It was featured in a food video that got upward of thirty million views, and because of that, I received nearly as many opinions on these contentious little suckers. Among the main objections? "They look like gummy worms, Linda. You're trying to trick us into eating vegetable candy, and that isn't cool." Umm, sorry? "Food coloring is the devil, and there is no way you can make those colors without it, so you are the devil, Linda." I hope this book is enough to refute that! And finally, "But they're so much work—no thanks!" That couldn't be further from the truth. They're among the easiest of shapes, in fact. Give them a go; you won't regret it. MAKES 4 SERVINGS

SPECIAL EQUIPMENT
A silicone sushi mat or a gnocchi board

⅙ batch Beet-Paprika Dough (page 63; red)
⅙ batch Harissa Dough (page 61; orange)
⅙ batch Turmeric Dough (page 56; yellow)
⅙ batch Leafy Greens Dough (page 51; green)
⅙ batch Spirulina Dough or Butterfly Pea Flower Dough
  (page 44 or 45; blue)
⅙ batch Beet-Blueberry Dough (page 40; purple)
Flour (and semolina, if needed) for dusting
Kosher salt

1. Roll out each ball of dough into a rectangle using the second-*thickest* setting on a pasta machine. Since this is still quite thick, it's very easy to use a rolling pin instead of a pasta machine if you wish. Take care that each color is roughly the same size.

2. Using a straight rolling cutter, cut each color of dough lengthwise into ½-inch strips.

3. Lay one red strip on your surface as a starting point. Next, lay an orange strip over the red strip, leaving ¼ inch of red exposed. Next, lay a yellow strip over

the orange, leaving ¼ inch of the orange exposed. Repeat next with the green, then the blue, and finally the purple strip.

4. At this point you should have a rainbow dough strip that is roughly 1½ inches wide. Continue making rainbow-colored strips until you have used all the remaining strips of dough.

5. Using a bench scraper or chef's knife, cut each rainbow strip crosswise into ¼ inch pieces. Sparingly flour these pieces of dough so that they do not stick to the sushi mat. If you over-flour the cavatelli, you'll lose some of the vibrancy of the rainbow pattern you worked so hard to achieve, so use just enough flour so the pasta doesn't stick to the mat.

6. TO SHAPE WITH A BENCH SCRAPER (PREFERRED): Use the cutting edge of the bench scraper to pull each piece of dough *toward yourself* across the sushi mat.

TO SHAPE WITH YOUR THUMB: Use the side of your thumb to roll each piece of dough *away from yourself* across the sushi mat.

7. In either case, apply enough pressure so that the dough curls around itself and grooves are formed, but not so much pressure that the dough sticks to the mat. If the dough is repeatedly sticking to the mat, flour it.

8. Repeat the process with the remaining pieces of dough. Let the cavatelli rest for 30 minutes or up to 2 hours at room temperature before boiling. If you would like to cook it another day, store the pasta on a parchment-lined and semolina-dusted sheet pan covered with plastic wrap in the refrigerator for up to 3 days. Increase the cooking time by 1 minute if working with refrigerated pasta.

9. Boil in salted water for 2 to 3 minutes or until floating, drain, dress, and serve immediately.

STARS PAPPARDELLE

I've used various types of cutters to make shapes in pasta, and when feasible I prefer to use plunger-style cutters because they really save the tips of my fingers from burning clean off after I've cut out about two hundred of the same shape. If you have only a metal cookie cutter, it will certainly work, but plunger cutters can be found inexpensively at most cooking or craft stores as well as online. As with all the patterns in this book, you don't need to cut the finished star sheets into pappardelle. Farfalle, lasagne sheets, or any other noodles on the larger side would also showcase this pattern well.   MAKES 4 SERVINGS

SPECIAL EQUIPMENT
A star-shaped plunger cutter

½ batch dough (your choice of color)
Flour and semolina for dusting
½ batch dough (your choice of color)
Kosher salt

1. Choose which color of dough you want to be the background color for your stars and roll that dough to the third-thinnest setting on a pasta machine. Lightly dust a work surface with flour and place the pasta sheet on it. Using a star-shaped plunger cutter in any size you prefer, make star cutouts all over the sheet of pasta. I recommend spacing the star cutouts as close together as possible, because the sheet will get re-rolled and the stars will expand (doesn't stars expanding blow your mind?). Cover this sheet with a kitchen towel. If you wish, save the tiny cutout stars to make pastina (page 78).

2. Roll the second dough on a pasta machine until it is the same size as the sheet with the star cutouts. Uncover the cutout pasta sheet and moisten it slightly with a kitchen brush dipped in water or a damp paper towel. Taking care to cover the cutout sheet precisely, lay the newly rolled sheet over the cutout sheet. Use a rolling pin to sandwich the two sheets together, rolling both lengthwise and crosswise.

3. Once you are sure the two sheets are sufficiently pressed together, use a bench scraper to carefully turn the pasta sheet over, revealing the star pattern. You may be able to make nips, tucks, and small

adjustments at this point if you notice any bunching up of the pattern. Dust with flour as necessary to prevent sticking.

4. Roll the sheet through the pasta machine again, starting on the widest setting. Reduce the rollers to the second-widest setting and roll the opposite end of the sheet through first this time. Alternating the sides of the sheet you put through the pasta machine will ensure that the stars don't skew too much in one direction. Keep reducing the rollers until you've rolled the pasta sheet through the middle thickness on the pasta machine. Your stars will look wide! Don't worry; we're about to fix that.

5. Lay the pasta sheet flat on your work surface and cut the whole sheet crosswise in 5-inch widths (or wider, up to the width of your pasta machine rollers). The star pattern has so far been skewed only side to side, making really wide stars, so now we'll run the 5-inch sheets *crosswise* through the pasta machine, to stretch the stars back toward symmetry.

6. Feed the 5-inch widths of pasta through the pasta machine crosswise this time, perpendicular to the direction you

had been feeding them through initially. Watch the star pattern and stop sheeting at your desired thinness, depending on how stretched or skewed you want the stars. I suggest stopping at the second- or third-thinnest setting.

7. Working with one sheet at a time, cut lengthwise strips ¾ to 1 inch wide. Hang the noodles to rest (see page 16) on a pasta drying rack, dowel, or the back of a chair and repeat the process with the remaining pasta sheets.

8. Let the pappardelle rest for 30 minutes hanging, then gently place them on a parchment-lined and semolina-dusted sheet pan. You can boil them at this point or wait up to 2 hours at room temperature before boiling. If you would like to cook them another day, after they are leathery to the touch and no longer sticky, store the pasta on a sheet pan covered with plastic wrap in the refrigerator for up to 3 days. Increase the cooking time by 1 minute if working with refrigerated pasta.

9. Boil in salted water for 2 minutes, drain, dress, and serve immediately.

POLKA-DOT FARFALLE

Farfalle lend themselves to all sorts of patterns—stripes, swirls, what have you—but polka dots, with their instant cheer and effortless exuberance, have to be one of my favorite patterns to adorn them. My son, Bentley Danger, whose pickiness about vegetables was a big impetus for me making colored pasta in the first place, is as fashionable as a kid in the ten-and-under set can get. His favorite accessory? The bow tie. His favorite bow tie? Bright green with white polka dots. Clearly it has had an impact on me, because here I am showing you how to make *meeeellions* more just like it.

You will need a utensil capable of punching small circles in dough for this recipe. You can use round plunger cutters in various sizes, from about ¼ inch in diameter on up to ⅔ inch. Any larger and the dots look more like blobs; any smaller and they sometimes close back up when sheeted. You can also use round pastry piping tips, which many people conveniently have floating in their junk drawers already. Don't assume that piping tips are the inferior choice; they are actually quite comfortable to slip over your fingers and punch away to your heart's content.

Keep in mind while rolling that your end goal is to have a long sheeted strip of dough that you will cut into smaller rectangles to shape into individual farfalle. You may make farfalle in any size, but 1½ by 2 inches is a good goal.

And I apologize in advance for the excessive use of the word *moist*. Doesn't it make you cringe? MAKES 4 SERVINGS

½ batch dough (your choice of color)
Flour for dusting
½ batch dough (your choice of color)
Kosher salt

1. Choose which dough color you want your polka dots to be. Keep that dough covered in plastic wrap and roll the *other* color out to the third-thinnest setting on a pasta machine. Take care that you sheet it into a rectangle as wide as the rollers on your pasta machine will allow, as you'll need to roll the second dough into the exact same shape.

2. Lightly flour the bottom of the rolled sheet and place it on your work surface. You may cut it in half if it is too long for your surface; just be sure to keep the reserved half covered under a kitchen towel so it doesn't dry out.

3. Using either round piping tips or plunger cutters, punch circles into the sheet of pasta, getting the holes about

½ inch apart from one another. I like to use two different-size piping tips, each on both my index fingers, because it goes faster using both hands and I like to vary the pattern. You can use the same size circles if you wish; just be sure to work quickly, as you don't want your dough to dry out. If you feel your dough is drying out, you can wipe it with a moistened and wrung-out paper towel to keep it from cracking. Once your entire sheet is punched, cover it with a kitchen towel.

4. Roll the other dough to the exact same size as the sheet with the holes in it. If you're off by ½ inch here or there, don't worry; you can pull and stretch this top sheet to the edges.

5. Uncover the hole-riddled sheet and wipe it all over with a moistened and wrung-out paper towel. The paper towel should be just moist enough to make the pasta slightly tacky, never dripping with water, or you'll have a soggy mess on your hands.

6. Working carefully so as not to crumple your sheet, lay the second sheet over the first, taking care to cover it as completely and precisely as you can. Smooth your hands over it to make sure there are no air pockets between the sheets and gently roll a pin over the sheets to ensure they are stuck together. Lightly flour the top of the second sheet.

7. Now you're ready for the big reveal! Using a bench scraper, very gently (in case the sheet sticks a bit to the counter surface) start at one end of the sheet and roll it back so that the polka-dot side is exposed. Use the bench scraper to gently dislodge any of the sheet that might have stuck to the counter, rather than tugging with your hands. When the entire polka-dot side is exposed, examine it for any tears or smooshes in the pattern and smooth what you can with your fingers.

8. Next you'll roll the sheets back through the pasta machine, using two methods to keep your polka dots nice and round:

Alternate the end of dough you feed into the pasta machine with every new pass through.

Press the pasta sheet from short edge to short edge (crosswise, not lengthwise like the machine pulls the sheet) with a rolling pin between machine feeds so that it doesn't get too skewed lengthwise.

9. Start with the widest setting on a pasta machine and roll the sheet down to the second-thinnest setting, or as thin as you want your farfalle, alternating which end you feed through first as you get thinner and using a rolling pin crosswise as necessary. With each new roll, reexamine the pattern to make sure it is not tearing and the holes are not closing up.

10. Now you'll cut the farfalle. Work with 2 feet of pasta sheet at a time, with the rest covered under a kitchen towel to ensure it doesn't dry out. Using a rolling cutter, cut the sheet into rectangles that are about 1½ by 2 inches. I like to cut the long (2-inch) sides of the farfalle with a straight rolling cutter and the short (1½-inch) sides with a fluted cutter, to more closely resemble butterfly wings. On the other hand, if I'm trying to play up the bow tie rather than the butterfly angle, I use a straight rolling cutter for all of the cuts.

11. Position the rectangles so that a longer side faces you.

12. SHAPING OPTION 1: Place your thumb and forefinger on the bottom middle and center of a pasta rectangle and slide your thumb up toward your forefinger to make the first pinch, as shown opposite. Now lift your forefinger to the top middle of the rectangle and pull the top toward your thumb so that the resulting farfalla is pleated and gently pinched in the middle.

SHAPING OPTION 2: Place your forefinger on the center, your thumb on the bottom middle, and your middle finger on the top middle of the farfalla. Bring your middle finger and thumb inward toward your forefinger in one gentle pinching motion and release when the farfalla is pleated and pinched in the middle.

13. Repeat the process with the remaining dough. Let the farfalle rest for 30 minutes or up to 2 hours at room temperature before boiling. If you would like to cook them another day, after they are leathery to the touch and no longer sticky, store the pasta on a sheet pan covered with plastic wrap in the refrigerator for up to 3 days. Increase the cooking time by 1 minute if working with refrigerated pasta.

14. Boil in salted water for 1 to 2 minutes, drain, dress, and serve immediately.

HEARTS AND STRIPES PAPPARDELLE

Make this pappardelle when you want to show someone a little love in the form of carby color. It consists of two colors underneath, with a heart overlay. It's a loved-up trio you could use to celebrate your favorite sports team, Independence Day (hello, red, white, and blue), or any other color-themed occasion you can dream up. While I use a heart cutter, this technique will work with any cutter design you wish, such as flowers, stars, diamonds, or even fruit.   MAKES 4 SERVINGS

SPECIAL EQUIPMENT
A heart-shaped, ½- to 1-inch-diameter plunger cutter (or any other design you want)

⅓ batch dough (heart stripes: your choice of color)
Flour and semolina for dusting
⅓ batch dough (heart stripes: your choice of color)
½ batch dough (background: your choice of color)
Kosher salt

1. Roll one ⅓ batch of dough to the third-thinnest setting on a pasta machine. Lightly dust your work surface with flour and place the pasta sheet on it. Roll the second ⅓ batch of dough to the third-thinnest setting and cut it into strands using the fettuccine cutter attachment.

2. Moisten the first pasta sheet with a kitchen brush dipped in water or a damp paper towel. Lay the fettuccine strands lengthwise along the base sheet with ⅓ inch between them. Use a straight rolling cutter to trim any edge strands of fettuccine off the now-striped sheet, then gently press a rolling pin over the sheet to hold the design in place.

3. Run the striped sheet through the pasta machine starting at the widest setting and moving down to the third-thinnest. Cover the sheet with a kitchen towel.

4. Roll the ½ batch of dough through the pasta machine until it has the same dimensions as the striped sheet. Use a heart-shaped plunger cutter to cut hearts in the pasta sheet. You can cut hearts randomly across the pasta sheet or be more regimented about it, depending on if you want your final pappardelle to have heart smatterings or defined lines. Regardless, cut the hearts as close to one another as possible.

5. Uncover the striped sheet and very lightly dampen it with a kitchen brush dipped in water or a wet paper towel. Turn it over so that the stripes are facing down toward the heart cutout sheet and align the two sheets. Be sure the pattern is facedown so that the stripes will show through the heart cutouts. Gently place the striped sheet on top of the heart sheet and press out any bumps with your fingers. Lightly press a rolling pin over the sheets to affix them together.

6. When you're sure the sheets are sufficiently pressed together, use a bench scraper to carefully turn the pasta sheet

over, revealing the hearts and stripes pattern. You may be able to make nips, tucks, and small adjustments at this point if you notice any bunching up of the pattern. Dust with flour as necessary to prevent sticking.

7. Roll the sheet through the pasta machine again, starting on the widest setting. Reduce the rollers to the second-widest setting and roll the opposite end of the sheet through first this time, then reduce and roll again until the pasta sheet has been rolled through the middle thickness on the pasta machine. Alternating the sides of the sheet you put through the pasta machine will ensure that the hearts don't skew too much in just one direction.

8. Lay the pasta sheet flat on your surface and cut the whole sheet crosswise into 5-inch widths (or wider, up to the width of your pasta machine rollers) down the entire length. The heart pattern has so far been skewed only side to side, making really wide hearts, so now we'll run the 5-inch sheets *crosswise* through the pasta machine, to stretch the hearts back toward symmetry.

9. Feed the 5-inch widths of pasta through the pasta machine crosswise this time, perpendicular to the direction you had been feeding them through initially. Watch the heart pattern and stop sheeting at your desired thinness, depending on how stretched or skewed you want the hearts. I suggest stopping at the second- or third-thinnest setting.

10. Working with one sheet at a time, cut lengthwise strips that are ¾ to 1 inch wide. Hang the noodles to rest (see page 16) on a pasta drying rack, dowel, or the back of a chair and repeat the process with the remaining sheets.

11. Let the pappardelle rest for 30 minutes hanging, then gently place them on a parchment-lined and semolina-dusted sheet pan. You can boil them at this point or wait up to 2 hours at room temperature before boiling. If you would like to cook them another day, after they are leathery to the touch and no longer sticky, store the pasta on a sheet pan covered with plastic wrap in the refrigerator for up to 3 days. Increase the cooking time by 1 minute if working with refrigerated pasta.

12. Boil in salted water for 2 minutes, drain, dress, and serve immediately.

BICOLORED FUSILLI

Fusilli aren't silly at all as a pasta shape; in fact they are quite serious. That is, serious about providing all sorts of nooks and crannies for sauce to nestle into, making for a seriously nuanced plate of pasta. I've found that with fusilli in particular, a generous pour of my preferred Italian red wine, Gattinara, helps me to channel just the right mindset. They're one of my favorite shapes to showcase one color on one side and a different color on another, because two tones amplify the retro telephone-cord look.

You'll need either a knitting needle or a metal kebab skewer. The diameter will determine the width of your fusilli tendrils. Feel free to use any size needle up to about ⅓ inch, as any larger might be hard to manage. If you have a wooden needle/skewer lying around, it will certainly work, but if you're able, use metal, as the pasta won't stick to it as with wood, and it will make things slightly easier. If the skewer/needle has an endcap that is larger than the cylinder, just roll your fusilli with that end hanging off the edge of the surface so it doesn't affect the needle's ability to roll evenly across the surface.

The first time you make fusilli, start with the suggested amount of dough in the recipe, which is quarter batches of each color; if you try to make more, chances are your dough will dry out before you finish rolling this unique shape. As written, this will make two servings of pasta. If you want to scale up eventually, I still recommend working with a total of a half batch of dough at a time and sheeting new dough as you want more. This will prevent you from having an unmalleable sheet of dried-out pasta.

MAKES 2 SERVINGS

¼ batch dough (your choice of color)
¼ batch dough (your choice of color)
Flour for dusting
Kosher salt

1. Roll each color of dough to the third-thinnest setting on a pasta machine, taking care that the sheets are the same size as one another and as wide as your pasta machine rollers will allow. Flour the bottom of one sheet of pasta and lay it on your work surface, unfloured side up. Lay the second sheet of pasta on top of the first, doing your best to match it to the shape of the base sheet exactly. Flour the top of the second sheet. Gently roll the two sheets together, first with a rolling pin, then with a pasta machine. When the bicolored sheet is through the third-thinnest pasta machine setting, it's ready to become fusilli.

2. Using a straight rolling cutter, cut the pasta sheet crosswise into four pieces. Work with a quarter sheet of pasta at a time, keeping the remaining sheets covered with a kitchen towel to prevent drying. Cut the jagged end off your quarter sheet so that you have a pasta rectangle. Lightly flour this sheet so that it does not stick to the skewer when twisting.

3. Using the same rolling cutter, cut the sheet crosswise into noodles that are ¼ to ½ inch wide and 5 to 6 inches long. Work with one noodle at a time. Place a noodle on the work surface on a diagonal and wrap the near end of it around your skewer, about halfway up the needle. Position your open palm across the skewer/needle on top of where you've wrapped the noodle and roll away from you gently against the work surface. This will result in the noodle twisting around the skewer in a spiral.

4. Gently slide the noodle off the skewer, taking care not to rip or snag it. If you notice that it wants to bond to the skewer, add a little more flour to the remaining noodles. Winding the noodles too tightly around the skewer can also result in them sticking. When you move

your palm across the surface, do so with just enough pressure to get the noodle and skewer to roll. Don't apply so much pressure that the noodle smooshes into the skewer.

5. Repeat to make the remaining fusilli, taking care to give each its own space on the work surface.

6. Let the fusilli rest for at least 45 minutes or up to 2 hours at room temperature before boiling. If you would like to cook them another day, after they are leathery to the touch and no longer sticky, store the pasta on a sheet pan covered with plastic wrap in the refrigerator for up to 3 days. Increase the cooking time by 1 minute if working with refrigerated pasta.

7. Boil in salted water for 1 to 2 minutes, drain, dress, and serve immediately.

ARGYLE LASAGNE SHEETS

There's something so satisfying about argyle as a pattern. It's a classic that looks good on everything from sweaters to socks to, you guessed it, pasta. You do not necessarily have to make a baked lasagna out of these sheets. Instead, you could serve them tossed with a little browned butter. After all, you worked so hard to make them; they might as well be the star of the show, not buried beneath layers of Bolognese. You could also make just a few and use them as the top layer of a lasagna with the sauce and cheese tucked beneath. MAKES 4 SERVINGS

SPECIAL EQUIPMENT
A diamond-shaped cookie cutter, about 1¾ inches long

½ batch dough (base color: your choice of color)
Flour for dusting
¼ batch dough (your choice of color)
¼ batch dough (your choice of color)
¼ batch dough (your choice of color)
Kosher salt (if pre-boiling)

1. Roll the ½ batch of dough to the third-thinnest setting on a pasta machine, making sure it is as wide a sheet as the pasta machine rollers will allow. Flour the bottom of the sheet and cover it with a kitchen towel. This is your base sheet.

2. Roll two of the ¼ batches of dough to the second-thinnest setting on a pasta machine. Using the diamond-shaped cutter, cut as many diamonds out of both of the ¼ batches of dough as you can. Work as quickly as you can to keep the diamonds from drying out.

3. Uncover the base sheet of pasta and lightly moisten it all over with a damp paper towel. Lay alternating colors of

diamonds across the base sheet in rows, one adjacent to the next crosswise. Once you've covered the entire sheet with

in the centers of the diamonds, forming a crisscross pattern. You may run out of strands, which is why you have the second pasta sheet waiting to be cut into spaghetti strands if needed. I advise against cutting it all at once so that it doesn't dry out too quickly.

6. At this point your argyle pattern is complete. I prefer to use a rolling pin to flatten the sheet of pasta to my desired thinness, because if you place this sheet back in the pasta machine, you risk distorting your pattern. To make the sheet easier to press together with the rolling pin, use a straight rolling cutter to trim the thin spaghetti strands that extend beyond the base sheet of pasta. If you roll it by hand from this point, you can roll it both lengthwise and crosswise until it's flattened to your desired thinness,

pasta diamonds, gently press them to the base sheet with a rolling pin. Cover this sheet with a kitchen towel.

4. Roll the final ¼ batch of dough out to the second-thinnest setting on a pasta machine. Divide the pasta sheet in half crosswise and cut one half into spaghetti-thin strands using the spaghetti-cutter attachment on a pasta machine. Reserve the other half under a kitchen towel.

5. Uncover the base diamond sheet and moisten it with a kitchen towel (as needed). Begin laying the strands of spaghetti diagonally in one direction across the sheet, with the strands passing diagonally through the centers of the diamonds. When an entire direction of diagonal strands is complete, lay strands across the base sheet in the opposite diagonal direction. The strands should intersect

while also being mindful not to stretch the diamonds too wide and mar the pattern.

7. On the other hand, if you're open to a certain amount of pattern skewing, you may run the sheet back through the pasta machine to your desired thinness; just be sure to start on a very wide setting so that your pattern doesn't get caught and torn in the machine.

8. When cutting this argyle sheet into lasagne noodles, keep the pattern in mind so that you can fully visualize the argyle on the finished product. I like to use a fluted rolling cutter and first cut along all of the outer edges to lend the fluted effect, then cut crosswise through the middle of every other diamond, to create lasagne sheets that are about 3 inches wide.

9. Let the lasagne sheets rest for 30 minutes or up to 2 hours at room temperature before boiling. If you would like to cook them another day, after they are leathery to the touch and no longer sticky, store the pasta on a sheet pan covered with plastic wrap in the refrigerator for up to 3 days.

10. If you're layering these sheets into an actual lasagna, pre-boiling the sheets is optional. The benefit is that the pasta will absorb less moisture from the sauce, making for a saucier lasagna, but on the other hand the lasagne sheets won't stay as firm. It's a matter of textural preference. If you choose to pre-cook them, boil the sheets one at a time in salted water for 15 seconds and lay them flat on a drying rack to cool, before layering them into lasagna. If you're not using them in a lasagna but rather to be tossed with sauce, boil in salted water for 1 to 2 minutes, drain, dress, and serve immediately.

MULTICOLORED GARGANELLI

Some people describe garganelli as penne you can make by hand, but I feel that description does a disservice to this shape, which is so much more. For one thing, it's just as pretty as can be, whereas a mass of penne looks like a pile of severed pens. For another, the groovy texture of garganelli and the crisp tips at the ends beckon sauce in a way penne never could, making garganelli a go-to pasta for rich, clingy sauces, such as Pork Shoulder Braised in Milk and Rosé with Figs (page 242).

The word *garganelli* comes from an Emilia-Romagnan dialect version of a word that means "chicken esophagus," presumably because of the ribbed texture and the slender shape. The garganelli pictured here take advantage of one of my favorite concepts in all of Italian cuisine: *cucina povera,* a.k.a. don't waste a damn thing. That's because they're made from a mess of scraps from your other pasta endeavors. I save pasta scraps in plastic wrap from a few days of pasta making, then re-sheet the scraps all together, which results in patterns that can never be replicated. That's truly once-in-a-lifetime pasta. Garganelli is a good shape to make with scraps because as pasta gets worked, it gets tougher, and garganelli benefit from a bit of rigidity in the dough to maintain their tubular form.

If you don't have scraps, no problem. You can make garganelli out of a single color of fresh dough; just be sure to laminate it thoroughly (see page 72) so it's nice and stiff when shaped. If you still want the multicolored, random look, break off pieces of different colors of dough and ball them together in a clump before rolling and sheeting.

MAKES 4 SERVINGS

SPECIAL EQUIPMENT
A silicone sushi mat or a gnocchi board
5/16-inch-diameter dowel (about the length of a pencil) or a clean round pencil
A ruler (optional, but helpful if you are obsessed with precision)

Pasta scraps saved from other pasta endeavors, totaling the equivalent of 1 batch of pasta dough (see Note, page 134)
Flour for dusting
Kosher salt

1. Work with ½ batches of dough at a time to ensure the pasta doesn't dry out before you can shape it.

2. Sheet the dough 4½ inches wide to the second-thinnest setting on a pasta machine. When you're sheeting scraps together, it's useful to first roll them together with a rolling pin, being mindful to keep the colors you want to see facing upward as you sheet and laminate the dough. If you laminate the dough too much and you're using many different colors, they will bleed into one another and go muddy. If you want to keep some of the colors distinct, don't fold the dough onto itself too many times; after all, it's already been worked—it's a scrap.

3. Using a straight rolling cutter, cut ¼ inch off both long sides of the pasta sheet. This will give you a clean 4-inch-wide pasta sheet. Use the cutter to cut the sheet lengthwise directly down the middle. Now, you should have two strips that are each 2 inches wide. Cut each strip into 2-inch pieces, so that you wind up with 2-inch squares. There is a fancy tool called a pasta bike that can make short work of cutting precise squares of pasta, but unless you're certifiably obsessed, don't worry too much if you're a tiny bit off on your square-cutting ninja skills.

4. Place the sushi mat on the surface directly in front of you, take up your ~~sword~~ dowel, and prepare to ~~battle~~ shape the garganelli. Wrap one corner of a pasta square around the middle of a dowel and rest it so that the dowel is perpendicular to the grooves on your mat and the dowel is at the pasta square corner closest to you. With gentle pressure, roll the dowel away from you until the pasta is completely wrapped around it. Slide your masterpiece off the dowel and repeat with the remaining squares. If you're having trouble with the pasta sticking to the dowel, lightly flour it. Don't use too much flour, though, or you risk the pasta becoming too dry to stick to itself.

5. Let the garganelli rest for 45 minutes or up to 2 hours at room temperature before boiling. If you would like to cook them another day, after they are leathery to the touch and no longer sticky, store the pasta on a sheet pan covered with plastic wrap in the refrigerator for up to 3 days. Increase the cooking time by 1 minute if working with refrigerated pasta.

6. Boil in salted water for 1 to 2 minutes, drain, dress, and serve immediately.

NOTE: *Use only scraps that have been sealed in plastic wrap and aren't excessively dry and brittle to start with. If you don't have an entire batch's worth, don't fret; make less and serve appetizer portions, or even make a small amount to boil up just for you. After all, the chef deserves a special solo treat after slaving away in the kitchen all day. In professional kitchens that's known as the chef's reward, and while it often refers to the hidden "oyster" portion on a roasted chicken, I don't see why a personal batch of pasta can't be considered a worthy equivalent.*

CANNELLONI RIGATI

If you see the word *rigati* or *rigate* attached to a pasta shape, it just means that it has lines (*righe* in Italian) on it. The lines, or grooves, help sauce adhere to the noodles, but to be honest, that's not why I'm showing you cannelloni with lines on it. It's because this can be a tricky shape to master, and one of the biggest snafus happens when the pasta sheet sticks to the dowel you're rolling it around. Rolling it against a ridged surface rather than a smooth one gives the pasta something to stick to on the other side of the sheet, which keeps it from sticking to the dowel and making a mess of your hard-earned pasta.

I'll explain how to make cannelloni using single-colored dough, and I suggest you master that first. After you've rolled tubes upon tubes upon tubes and you want to go crazy making patterns and splashing color onto those designs, have at it—but for now, let's stick to technique.

You'll need some special tools for this shape, but lucky for you, none of it is expensive or particularly difficult to find. First off, let's talk dowels. If you already have some ¾-inch-diameter dowels for drying pasta for other recipes, you're one step ahead of the game. To dry enough cannelloni for four people, you'll need three 4-foot dowels. If you have only two, you can rotate the drier cannelloni off the dowels; it's really just important that the tubes dry on dowels until they're firm enough to keep their shape.

In addition to those drying dowels, you'll also need a shorter dowel—about 1 foot long—that is ⅞ inch in diameter, or a little larger in diameter than your drying dowels. If you have to buy an entire 4-foot length and cut it down, don't lament too much. I wind up using my foot-long dowels for rolling, hanging, and draping all the time.

One final note before we dive in: Cannelloni is incredible when filled and baked; use any filling in the book except the *egg yolk filling*. The best way to go about it is to boil the cannelloni for 30 seconds, drain them, and pipe filling inside. Then they can be baked as you would any baked pasta. Alternatively, you can boil the cannelloni for the entire cooking time and fill them with an already-hot filling; just take care not to burn your fingers. Because they're usually filled with something hearty, and often sauced to boot, one batch of dough will probably make more than 4 servings. Nevertheless, I recommend sheeting one entire batch the first time, to get the hang of it and so that you don't worry so much if a few pieces go south. If you do wind up with extra, you won't be disappointed. MAKES 4 SERVINGS

SPECIAL EQUIPMENT
A silicone sushi mat or a gnocchi board (see Note, page 139)
1 rolling dowel, ⅞-inch diameter, 1 foot long
2 or more drying dowels, ¾-inch diameter, 4 feet long
Kitchen scissors (sharp and small)

1 batch dough (your choice of color) or the equivalent of 1 batch dough
    composed of several different colors
Flour and semolina for dusting
Kosher salt

1. Work with ¼ batch of dough at a time and keep the remaining dough wrapped in plastic. As you get faster at this process, you can experiment with working with more dough, but if you don't work quickly, the pasta sheets will dry out before you've had a chance to form the cannelloni.

2. Roll the dough in a rectangular shape about 5 inches wide to the third-thinnest setting on a pasta machine. Place the sushi mat on a work surface directly in front of you with the grooves running parallel to the counter edge. Place the pasta sheet directly behind the mat, or nearby where you can easily access and cut it.

3. Place the ⅞-inch rolling dowel along one short edge of the pasta sheet, and wrap the pasta around the dowel. When the pasta is wrapped completely around the dowel, eyeball about ½ inch extra and use a straight rolling cutter to cut that entire piece away from the main sheet.

4. At this point you have two options. You can either use that piece as a template and cut the remaining pasta sheet into individual rectangles the same size, or you can repeat the roll-and-cut process each time. I advise you to repeat the roll-and-cut process each time as you get some good cannelloni-making skills under your belt, because the pasta can shrink if you don't get to it quickly enough, thus ruining your future cannelloni, and

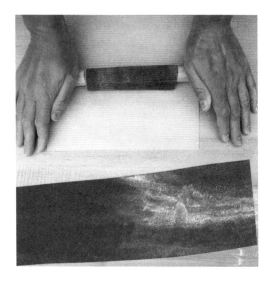

6. When you have the pasta wrapped entirely around the dowel and the seam is on the bottom, touching the mat, begin pressing down and continue to roll toward yourself until you have rolled ridges onto the entire pasta tube. Look at where the edge of the dough comes together and make sure it is fully crimped. If it's not, you can roll it again to ensure that your tube remains a tube.

7. Gently slide one edge of the newly formed cannellone (singular) off the rolling dowel and snip the edge with the kitchen scissors to clean up the edge (or don't, if you're going for a rustic look). Slide the cannellone back onto the dowel and then slide it off the other end of the dowel, repeating the edge-snipping process for a cannellone that is about 4 inches long. Slide the cannellone off

also because cutting it prematurely contributes to it drying out—you guessed it, potentially ruining your future cannelloni. Once you get so speedy the Canadians nickname you Fasta Pasta, go ahead and try the template method.

5. Lightly flour the inside of the piece of pasta that is to become your cannelloni. Too much flour and your pasta won't crimp into a tube; too little and it will stick to the dowel. Place the pasta rectangle on the center rear portion of the mat, with the long edge of the pasta rectangle running the same direction as the grooves. Place the rolling dowel at the rear edge of the pasta rectangle and begin rolling the pasta rectangle toward you around the dowel without pressing down into the grooves.

the dowel completely and onto the drying dowel.

8. Repeat to make the remaining cannelloni, re-sheeting the reserved dough as necessary. Dry on the dowels until firm enough to hold their shape, about 30 minutes. Do not be tempted to store them on the dowels for more than 1 hour, as if they fully dry, the dowels will cause them to crack. Remove them from the dowels and place them on a parchment-lined and semolina-dusted sheet pan. Store them at room temperature for 4 hours or in the refrigerator covered with plastic wrap for up to 3 days.

9. Boil in salted water for 2 to 3 minutes, drain, dress, and serve immediately.

VARIATIONS

After you've mastered rolling this shape on the sushi mat, try it without the mat for a smooth version. It's undeniably harder to do, because the inside of the cannelloni is more tempted to stick to the dowel without something grabbing the exterior, but I have confidence in your abilities. Play around, you'll get it.

Experiment with turning the mat 90 degrees when you roll the cannelloni, resulting in ridges that are crosswise, not lengthwise. This makes for cannelloni that look just like tin cans, if you really want to get punny with your presentation.

On page 144 you'll find instructions for how to make paccheri, a shorter version of cannelloni that's not usually served stuffed.

NOTE: *Do not use a bamboo sushi mat; the twine that binds the bamboo tightly together will cut into your cannelloni. You can use a gnocchi board if you have a really giant one, but if you don't and you're going to buy one ridged item for all your pasta endeavors, I recommend the silicone sushi mat above all else for its versatility and practicality.*

RIGATONI

Rigatoni are among the most common tubed pasta shapes, and for good reason. Their medium size lends them to a wide variety of pasta dishes, ranging the spectrum from baked to boiled. Typically rigatoni are extruded, or pushed, through a machine and formed through specially shaped brass dies. Since most of us don't have expensive pasta extruders lying around, here's that meditative by-hand option. Bonus: No extruded rigatoni is going to come in endless color and pattern possibilities, proving that man is still slightly ahead of machine in that age-old science-fiction battle.

Rigatoni have ridges that run lengthwise along the tubes, but if you alter these directions slightly and roll your pasta tubes diagonally across the sushi mat instead, you can make a cool shape called elicoidali, which looks just like rigatoni except for the diagonal stripes. Elicoidali is named for helicoid, which literally means having the form of a flattened helix (yes, I'm an etymologist at heart).

I recommend reading the headnote for the cannelloni technique on page 135 if you haven't made them yet, to familiarize yourself with the equipment and process for making tubed shapes. MAKES 4 SERVINGS

SPECIAL EQUIPMENT

A silicone sushi mat or a gnocchi board
1 rolling dowel, ½-inch diameter, 1 foot long
2 or more drying dowels, ⅓-inch diameter, 4 feet long
Kitchen scissors (sharp and small)

1 batch dough (your choice of color) or the equivalent of 1 batch dough composed of several different colors
Flour and semolina for dusting
Kosher salt

1. Work with ¼ batch of dough at a time and keep the remaining dough wrapped in plastic. As you get faster at this process, you can experiment with working with more dough; if you don't work quickly, the pasta sheets will dry out before you've had a chance to form the rigatoni.

2. Roll the dough in a rectangular shape about 5 inches wide to the third-thinnest setting on a pasta machine. Place the sushi mat on your surface directly in front of you with the grooves running parallel to the counter edge. Place the pasta sheet directly behind the mat or nearby where you can easily access and cut it.

3. Place the ½-inch rolling dowel along one short edge of the pasta sheet and wrap the pasta around the dowel. When the pasta has wrapped completely around the dowel, eyeball about ¼ inch extra and use a straight rolling cutter to cut that entire piece away from the main sheet.

4. At this point you have two options. You can either use that piece as a template and cut the remaining pasta sheet into individual rectangles the same size, or you can repeat the roll-and-cut process each time. Initially I advise you to repeat the roll-and-cut process each

time as you get some good rigatoni-making skills under your belt, because the pasta can shrink if you don't get to it quickly enough, thus ruining your future rigatoni.

5. Lightly flour the inside of the piece of pasta that is to become your tube. Too much flour and your pasta won't crimp; too little and it will stick to the dowel. Place the pasta rectangle on the center rear portion of the mat, with the long edge of the pasta rectangle running the same direction as the grooves. Place the rolling dowel at the rear edge of the pasta rectangle, and begin rolling the pasta rectangle toward you around the dowel without pressing down into the grooves.

6. When you have the pasta wrapped entirely around the dowel and the seam is on the bottom, touching the mat, begin pressing down and continue to roll toward yourself until you have rolled ridges onto the entire pasta tube. Look at where the edge of the dough comes together and make sure it is fully crimped. If it's not, you can roll it again to ensure that your tube remains a tube, but try not to roll it too much as it will stretch the tube, making the diameter wider than it's supposed to be.

7. Gently slide one-third of the newly formed tube off the rolling dowel and snip it clean off. This is your first rigatoni. Slide it onto the drying dowel to open both edges and maintain the tubular shape. Slide another one-third off the rolling dowel, snip, and slide onto the drying dowel. Repeat with the last piece.

At this point it should become clear that you get three rigatoni from each rolled tube you form. You can clean up any uneven edges by snipping them if you like, but part of the charm is knowing the pasta is homemade, so don't go too crazy obsessing over uniformity.

8. Repeat to make the remaining rigatoni, re-sheeting the reserved dough as necessary. Dry on the dowels until firm enough to hold their shape, about 15 minutes. Do not be tempted to store them on the dowels for more than 2 hours, as if they fully dry, the dowels will cause them to crack. Remove them from the dowels and place them on a parchment-lined and semolina-dusted sheet pan. Store them at room temperature for 4 hours or in the refrigerator covered with plastic wrap for up to 3 days.

9. Boil in salted water for 2 to 3 minutes, drain, dress, and serve immediately.

STRIPED PACCHERI RIGATI

The forming technique for paccheri is the same as that of cannelloni with one extra tiny step, so if you've already made cannelloni, you'll be an old pro at this. Not that I'm calling you old, because you're not. You're young, vibrant, and in need of some totally tubular rainbows in your life.

Most packaged paccheri does not have ridges, and you're welcome to try to make these without the sushi mat for a smooth look. The sushi mat does prevent the pasta from sticking to the rolling dowel, however, so if you roll them smooth against a flat surface, be sure to use plenty of flour to avoid sticky frustration.

I recommend reading the headnote for the cannelloni technique on page 135 if you haven't made them yet, to familiarize yourself with the equipment and process.

MAKES 4 SERVINGS

SPECIAL EQUIPMENT
A silicone sushi mat or a gnocchi board
1 rolling dowel, ⅞-inch diameter, 1 foot long
2 or more drying dowels, ¾-inch diameter, 4 feet long
Kitchen scissors (sharp and small)

½ batch Basic Mother Dough (page 55)
Tennis ball–size pieces of 6 different pasta dough flavors. For a classic
    rainbow, make Beet-Blueberry (page 40), Spirulina (page 44),
    Leafy Greens (page 51), Turmeric (page 56), Harissa (page 61), and
    Beet-Paprika (page 63).
Flour and semolina for dusting
Kosher salt

1. Work with half of the basic dough and half of each of the six dough flavors at a time. Remember that tackling too much pasta dough at once can lead to dough that dries out and cracks before you get a chance to use it, so start small and as you gain proficiency you can work with larger batches.

2. Roll the basic dough to a 5-inch-wide rectangle that is through the third-thinnest setting on a pasta machine and cover with a kitchen towel. Roll each of the colored doughs to the same length as the basic dough. Run each of the colored doughs through the fettuccine attachment of the pasta machine and keep the resulting strips close by.

3. Lay the basic sheet on the work surface in front of you and moisten it lightly with a kitchen brush dipped in water or a damp paper towel. Start with the long edge that is farthest from you and lay a strip of fettuccine along it. Repeat with the next color and the next, working in whichever color order you prefer—red-orange-yellow-green-blue-purple if you want a classic rainbow. You should be able to repeat each color at least three times by the time you reach the other edge of the pasta sheet.

4. Press the rainbow sheet along its length with a rolling pin to make sure all of the strips are sealed to the base sheet, then run it back through the pasta machine, starting at the widest setting on down to the third-thinnest setting.

5. Place the sushi mat on the work surface directly in front of you with the grooves running parallel to the counter edge. Place the pasta sheet directly behind the mat or nearby where you can easily access and cut it.

6. Place the ⅞-inch rolling dowel along one short edge of the pasta sheet and wrap the pasta around the dowel. When the pasta has wrapped completely around the dowel, eyeball about ½ inch extra and use a straight rolling cutter to cut that entire piece away from the main sheet.

7. At this point you have two options. You can either use that piece as a template and cut the remaining pasta sheet into individual rectangles the same size, or you can repeat the roll-and-cut process each time. Initially I advise you to repeat the roll-and-cut process each time, because the pasta can shrink if you don't get to it quickly enough, thus ruining your future paccheri, and also because cutting it prematurely contributes to it drying out—you guessed it, potentially ruining your future paccheri.

8. Lightly flour the inside of the piece of pasta that is to become your tube. Too much flour and your pasta won't crimp into a tube; too little, and it will stick to the dowel. Place the pasta rectangle on the center rear portion of the mat, with the long edge of the pasta rectangle running the same direction as the grooves. Place the rolling dowel at the rear edge of the pasta rectangle and begin rolling the pasta rectangle toward you around the dowel without pressing down into the grooves.

9. When you have the pasta wrapped entirely around the dowel and the seam is on the bottom, touching the mat, begin pressing down and continue to roll toward yourself until you have rolled ridges onto the entire pasta tube. Look at where the edge of the dough comes together and make sure it is fully crimped. If it's not, you can roll it again to ensure that your tube remains a tube.

10. Gently slide one edge of the newly formed tube off the rolling dowel and snip the edge with the kitchen scissors to clean up the edge (or don't, if you are going for a rustic look). Slide it a little farther down and snip it again, forming a shorter tube that is about 1½ inches

long. Repeat until you have three short tubes, trimming the end of the last tube if you wish for a clean edge. Slide the three paccheri onto the drying dowel.

11. Repeat with the rest of the pasta sheet, and then repeat from the beginning again, with the second half of the dough. Dry on the dowels until firm enough to hold their shape, about 20 minutes. Do not be tempted to store them on the dowels for more than 1 hour, as if they fully dry, the dowels will cause them to crack. Remove them from the dowels and stand them up vertically on a parchment-lined and semolina-dusted sheet pan until they are stiff enough to hold their shape. Then you can lay them down and store them at room temperature for 4 hours, or in the refrigerator covered with plastic wrap for up to 3 days. Increase the cooking time by 1 minute if working with refrigerated pasta.

12. Boil in salted water for 3 minutes, drain, dress, and serve immediately.

SMALL STRIPED AGNOLOTTI

When I want a lot of stuffed pasta, agnolotti is my go-to shape, because it's easy to form quickly and beautifully once you get the hang of it. There's something about the Zen rhythm of pinching together hundreds of tiny pasta pillows that soothes the soul, not just the stomach, so if you take the time to learn just one filled pasta technique, make it this one.

The technique shown here is technically called *agnolotti dal plin* in Piedmont, where they were born to the tune of angels rejoicing long, long ago. *Plin* means "pinch" in Piemontese dialect, and it refers to the fact that to seal each piece of pasta, you use your thumb and forefinger to pinch the pockets closed.

This agnolotti is striped, but you could make any color or pattern you choose, or none at all and just let the beauty lie in the precisely pinched parcels.   MAKES 4 SERVINGS

1 batch filling from chapter 6 (but not the burrata)
2/3 batch dough (your choice of color)
Flour and semolina for dusting
1/3 batch dough (your choice of color)
Kosher salt

1. Put the filling in a gallon-size zip-top bag or disposable piping bag and store in the refrigerator until needed.

2. Roll the 2/3 batch of dough out into a rectangle that is 4 inches wide and 2 feet long. This is the base sheet. Put it on a floured surface and cover with a kitchen towel.

3. Roll the 1/3 batch of dough to the third-thinnest setting on the pasta machine, or until it is at least 2 feet long. Flour this sheet and cut it into strands using the fettuccine cutter on the pasta machine. Take care to lay the strands flat on the work surface so that they don't tangle too much with one another or they may stick together.

4. Uncover the base sheet and wipe it with a just-damp paper towel or kitchen brush so that the strands will adhere to it. Lay the strands lengthwise along the sheet to make stripes, starting with the side closest to you and working your way back. Try to leave less than a ¼-inch gap between the strands, as the spaces will stretch out when you roll out the sheet. Be careful that the strands are flat and untangled and lay evenly across the sheet. Repeat until the base sheet is covered in stripes. Gently press the stripes onto the base sheet with a rolling pin, to ensure that they are adhered before sheeting with the pasta machine. Use a straight rolling cutter to trim any excess strands that extend beyond the base sheet.

5. Carefully roll the striped sheet out to the second-thinnest setting on a pasta machine. You may wish to cut it into two (or more) pieces as you sheet further, as it will make the sheets easier to handle, and you'll need to have room

for the sheets on your work surface to stuff them. Cover unused sheets with a kitchen towel to ensure they don't dry out.

6. Lay the pasta sheets on a lightly floured surface with the stripe pattern facing *down*. Observe the edge of the pasta sheet that is closest to you. If it is excessively dry or uneven, use a straight rolling cutter to clean up the edge. Use your finger to distribute a 1-inch line of flour along the entire front edge. This helps keep the filling from making the pasta sheet soggy.

1. Remove the bag of filling from the refrigerator and snip a 2/3-inch hole from a bottom corner. Starting about 1 inch in from the long edge of the pasta sheet, pipe a line of filling along the entire front edge, stopping about 1 inch from the end. Roll the front edge of the pasta sheet over the filling onto itself along the entire edge, so that you can no longer see the filling. Now roll it forward one more time.

2. Start at one end of the pasta filling tube and pinch 1-inch segments of the filling, using the thumb and forefinger of both hands as you work your way down the filling tube. When you reach the end, you'll often notice that the tube drops forward another partial turn onto itself, but if it doesn't droop over, don't worry, you can help it along in a moment.

3. By now, you should have a small lip of pasta sheet left all along the top edge. Some people keep this edge untrimmed and rustic, but for a classic agnolotti look, you can cut along the entire back edge with a fluted rolling cutter.

4. Finally, use the fluted rolling cutter to crimp and cut through every "pinch" along the length of the sheet. Your pinches provide the guide for where to cut, thus defining the final piece size of the agnolotti. As you get more proficient at agnolotti making, you can play with making 1/2-inch or even tinier agnolotti, or even go in the opposite direction and make enlarged versions.

5. Repeat with the remaining filling and pasta sheets until you run out of dough or filling or, ideally, both.

6. Let the agnolotti rest for 30 minutes or up to 2 hours at room temperature before boiling. You may also store the pasta on a parchment-lined and semolina-dusted sheet pan uncovered in the refrigerator for up to 8 hours. Increase the cooking time by 1 minute if working with refrigerated pasta.

7. Boil in salted water for 3 minutes, drain, dress, and serve immediately.

VARIATION

You can use two (or more) different colors of pasta for the stripes if you wish. Just alternate every other one if you want more color in the pattern.

It will take a bit longer, but you can run the stripes perpendicular instead of parallel along the base sheet. If you do this, be sure to get the strips of pasta really close together, as sheeting them down to the second-thinnest setting will really stretch them out.

LATTICE-PATTERNED CARAMELLE

Caramelle means "candies" in Italian, and this pasta shape is so named because it resembles a well-wrapped parcel of something splendid. I've always leaned more toward the savory side of life, so unwrapping a pretty pasta package is a welcome surprise. You can use any color or pasta pattern to make your caramelle, but I'm going to show you how to make a lattice pattern here, both because it looks neat and because it's not too hard, so you can focus your energy on mastering the caramelle-wrapping technique.

If you have another pattern in mind or want to make single-colored caramelle, skip down to the filling and shaping instructions after you've got your pasta sheet rolled and ready to fill.   MAKES 4 SERVINGS (3 CARAMELLE PER PERSON)

> 1 batch filling from chapter 6 (Classic Ricotta Filling, page 255; Rustic Squash Filling, page 258; or Taleggio Pear Filling, page 257, will work best)
> 2/3 batch dough (your choice of color)
> Flour and semolina for dusting
> 1/2 batch dough (your choice of color)
> Kosher salt

1. Put the filling in a gallon-size zip-top bag or disposable piping bag and put in the refrigerator until needed.

2. Roll the 2/3 batch of dough to the fourth-thinnest setting on a pasta machine in a rectangular shape that's about 5 inches wide. Lightly dust a work surface with flour and rest this base sheet on it, covered with a kitchen towel.

3. Roll the 1/2 batch of dough to the third-thinnest setting on a pasta machine. Cut it crosswise into thirds and work with one-third at a time, covering the remaining two-thirds with a kitchen towel.

This is to ensure that your dough does not prematurely dry out and become unusable.

4. Lightly flour the one-third sheet so it doesn't clump. Using the spaghetti (narrowest) cutter attachment on a pasta machine, cut the sheet into strands. Place the base sheet horizontally in front of you on a lightly floured surface. Place the spaghetti strands directly behind the base sheet so they're easy to access.

5. Wipe the whole base sheet with a barely damp paper towel or kitchen brush so that the strands will stick to it.

Begin laying strands diagonally across the base sheet, about ½ inch apart (or as far apart as you want your pattern, keeping in mind that it will stretch when you re-roll it through the pasta machine). You may have to continue to moisten the base sheet if you notice that the strands aren't sticking properly to it, though you don't want it too wet or you risk the pattern bleeding.

6. When you've laid strands across the whole base sheet in one direction, repeat with strands running the opposite diagonal direction, cutting additional spaghetti strands as necessary from the reserved dough. Continue to moisten the base sheet as necessary, but again, not excessively.

7. When the pattern is complete in both directions, lightly roll across it with a rolling pin to affix the strands in place. Cut the excess strands that extend beyond the edges of the sheet with a rolling cutter. If there are any sticky patches from too much water, lightly flour them so they don't stick to the pasta machine.

8. Cut the patterned sheet in half so it's not unruly to work with and cover half with a kitchen towel. Run the other half through the pasta machine very carefully. You don't want your pattern to skew too much, so start on the widest setting and very gradually roll the sheet to the second-thinnest setting, alternating which end of the sheet you feed each time. Repeat with the second sheet, then cover both sheets with a kitchen towel while you prepare to fill and shape the caramelle.

FILLING AND SHAPING

1. Remove the bag of filling from the refrigerator and snip a ½-inch hole from a bottom corner. Work with one pasta sheet at a time. Lay the sheet in front of you on a work surface with the pattern side *down*. Dust the middle 2 inches of the pasta sheet with flour all the way down the length of the sheet to keep the filling from making the pasta soggy.

Starting at one short edge of the pasta sheet and working your way along it, pipe a 2-inch line of filling perpendicular to the length of the sheet, centering the filling. Roll the short edge of the pasta sheet around the filling and once it's covered, use a straight rolling cutter to cut 1 inch beyond that. Roll the sheet once more over your extra 1 inch.

2. Pinch the resulting caramella on either side of the filling to make a classic candy shape. At this point you can either cut the side edges of the caramella with a fluted rolling cutter, or if you like the rustic look, keep them as is.

3. Repeat with the remaining filling and pasta until you run out of dough or filling or, ideally, both.

4. Let the caramelle rest for 30 minutes or up to 2 hours at room temperature before boiling. You may also store the pasta on a parchment-lined and semolina-dusted sheet pan uncovered in the refrigerator for up to 8 hours. Increase the cooking time by 1 minute if working with refrigerated pasta.

5. Boil in salted water for 3 minutes, drain, dress, and serve immediately.

VARIATIONS

You can use two (or more) different colors of pasta for the stripes if you wish. Just alternate every other one if you want more color in the lattice pattern.

You can use fettuccine-thickness noodles for the stripes instead of the thinner noodles shown here. It will make a thicker lattice and reveal less of the base color.

Rather than pinching the caramelle shut on both sides, you can give each side a twist as you would the wrappers for those starlight peppermints you see at the hostess stand in restaurants.

CULURGIONES

This pinched packet of pasta is not for the pusillanimous. It's one of the trickier shapes to master, but boy, when you do, it's one of the most satisfying to both eat and gaze lovingly upon. The word *culurgiones* originated in Sardinian dialect, which is why it sounds so unlike other Italian words, not to mention ends in an "s." The shape is formed to resemble a grain of wheat, and the dialect roughly translates to "little bundles."

Classic culurgiones filling is potato-based, often with one of the many pecorino cheeses that are stars of Sardinia. You may choose any of the fillings in chapter 6 (except the burrata), but you'll want to make the filling on the stiff side, as a runny filling will make it impossible to complete the pinches properly. If you're really dying to try out the technique but you're feeling filling fatigue, you can cheat and stuff these with mozzarella *ciliegine*, a.k.a. the tiniest mozzarella balls you can find.   MAKES 4 SERVINGS

SPECIAL EQUIPMENT
A 3-inch round cutter

1 batch filling from chapter 6 (but not the burrata)
1 batch dough (your choice of color) or the equivalent of 1 batch dough composed of several different colors
Flour and semolina for dusting
Kosher salt

1. Put the filling in a gallon-size zip-top bag or disposable piping bag and put in the refrigerator until needed.

2. Work with ¼ batch of dough at a time and keep the remaining dough wrapped in plastic. As you get faster at this process, you can experiment with working with more dough, but if you don't work quickly, the pasta sheets will dry out

before you've had a chance to form the culurgiones.

3. Roll the dough to the second-thinnest setting on a pasta machine. Use the round cutter to cut out as many circles from the dough as you can. You may collect the leftover dough scraps and re-sheet them through the pasta machine to use again.

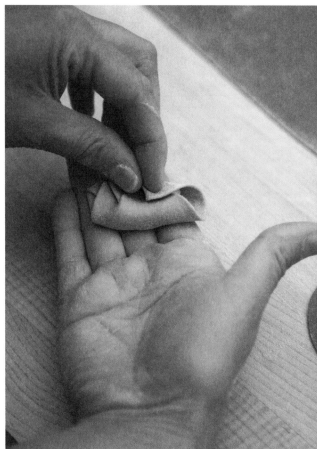

FILLING AND SHAPING

1. Remove the bag of filling from the refrigerator and snip a ½-inch hole from a bottom corner. Pipe a teaspoon-size dollop of filling in the shape of a teardrop into the middle of each circle. Don't get the skinny end of the teardrop closer than ½ inch from any edge. Working one at a time, pick up a circle and place it in the palm of your non-dominant hand. Fold the bottom lip of the circle up over the fat section of the filling, pressing the pasta into it to keep the pasta in place. Working from bottom-to-top, begin pulling small sections of each side of the circle in toward the middle, alternating pinching from side to side as though you were zipping the bundle closed. Continue this all the way up to the top of the bundle, and pinch the final tip to keep any filling from leaking out.

2. I've seen a Sardinian culurgiones expert get what seems like dozens of pinches in, but I'm happy if I get eight, as long as my bundle stays closed. Your first few may wind up on the scrap heap, but don't lose heart. Practice makes perfect when shaping culurgiones, and very soon you'll be pinching and pleating like a pasta boss. Start with just a few, and it will give you a good sense of how much filling to use and how to pipe it. Too much and it squeezes out the top, whereas too little will result in flat, wonky culurgiones. Keep a towel on hand to wipe filling off your fingers so they are as clean and dexterous as possible for shaping.

3. Repeat with the remaining filling and pasta until you run out of dough or filling or, ideally, both.

4. Let the culurgiones rest for 30 minutes or up to 2 hours at room temperature before boiling. You may also store the pasta on a parchment-lined and semolina-dusted sheet pan uncovered in the refrigerator for up to 8 hours. Increase the cooking time by 1 minute if working with refrigerated pasta.

5. Boil in salted water for 3 minutes, drain, dress, and serve immediately.

EMOJI RAVIOLONI

The good news is that this project can be as simple or as complex as you want it to be. A plain heart is an emoji, but so is the flamenco dancer, and try as I might, I've just never been able to master her elaborate shape, at least not with pasta as both ink and canvas. These days many cookie cutter makers have gotten in on the emoji action, so you can find cutters to make various shapes, but I've freehanded many of the more popular faces, foods, and of course poop, so don't feel as if you need to buy something special for each emoji.

These ravioli, or more accurately ravioloni, which just means that they're giant rav, are meant to serve one person apiece. A fun party involves making several of your favorite emoji faces, such as happy, kissy, angry, or laugh-cry, then inviting several friends over to duke it out over whose personality best suits which emoji. You can literally eat your feelings. They're also super fun for kids' parties, and if you serve them in that setting, I've learned from experience that you absolutely must include the poop emoji (don't worry, the brown comes from cacao dough).

If you do decide to use emoji cutters to make your designs, I recommend 2- to 3-inch cutters. Any larger than that and the design won't fit well on a one-person raviolone; any smaller and it will be too miniature to see, not to mention tricky to execute.

Bear in mind that most emoji cutters are made for use with cookies, so you may get the basic outline but you'll still have to fill in some details with individual strands of pasta. I'll illustrate that point with the peace sign emoji, which I happen to have a cutter for and which looks like a hand holding up two fingers.

After you've cut out a yellow or flesh-toned hand using the peace cutter, in order for the design to emerge you'll need to outline the hand and define the thumb and two littlest fingers with a thin noodle in a darker color made with brown (cacao) or black (charcoal) dough. To get the outline to stay in place, all you need is a steady hand and a clean, food-grade paintbrush to dab water on the base sheet where you want your outline strand to stick.

FILLINGS FOR EMOJI RAVIOLONI

With good planning, emoji ravioloni are not hard to make, but there are some things to plan that will really set you up for success. One is to consider the filling. From this book, three fillings will work well, listed below in order of difficulty from easiest to hardest to make and work with:

Burrata Filling (page 259)
Pepperoni Pizza Filling (page 260)
Egg Yolk Ravioloni (page 263)

Choose one based on the time you have and the vibe you're after. If you want to focus your energy on making the designs, not the filling, buy some balls of burrata and be done with it.

SPECIAL EQUIPMENT

FONDANT CUTTERS: One thing that makes pasta designs easier in general is investing in a fondant cutter set. They are inexpensive (generally less than $20) and come with cutters such as hearts, stars, flowers, and other shapes. I think outside the box with these—for example, the petals from a flower cutout can be cut into smaller pieces to make a teardrop. This is not essential, but it will make pasta patterns a little easier, and it's much less expensive to buy these cutters in a big set as opposed to individually, even if there's something in the set you think you won't use.

FOOD-SAFE PAINTBRUSHES: Have a few smaller-size brushes on hand resting in a jar of water to help you stick pasta to other pasta.

CLEAN KITCHEN SCISSORS: The smaller and sharper the better.

TWEEZERS: These can help with placing tiny pieces of pasta onto other pasta, although they aren't strictly necessary.

ROUND COOKIE CUTTERS: Ideally purchase a set, as you'll use sizes from 2 to 5 inches.

ROUND PIPING TIPS: These make great tools for cutting out tiny circles like eyeballs and pupils.

INGREDIENTS AND DOUGH COLORS

Before tackling emojis, look carefully at the ones you want to make. It helps to work from larger emoji images (easily searchable online) rather than the tiny ones on your phone keypad. I tend to always use Basic Mother Dough (page 55) as my base pasta sheet because the other colors show up well against it. If you want a different background color, be certain that whatever emojis you're making will pop against that color.

Here we'll tackle the heart, laugh-cry, poop, and pizza. I chose these four designs because they are different enough from one another that they cover a breadth of techniques that should help you to tackle many of the other emojis.

The first step is to write down the list of dough colors you'll need to make for the emojis chosen. For heart, laugh-cry, poop, and pizza, the lists look like this:

HEART
Basic Mother Dough (page 55)
Color of heart (red: Beet-Paprika, page 63)
Outline of heart (optional; either the same color as the heart or black: Activated Charcoal, page 43)

LAUGH-CRY
Basic Mother Dough (page 55)
Round face (yellow: Turmeric, page 56)
Face lines (your choice: Cacao for brown, page 46, or Activated Charcoal for black, page 43)
Inside of mouth (white: Milk, page 54)
Tears (blue: Butterfly Pea Flower, page 45; or Spirulina, page 44)

POOP
Basic Mother Dough (page 55)
Poop shape (brown: Cacao, page 46)
Poop eyes (white: Milk, page 54)
Poop eye pupils (black: Activated Charcoal, page 43)

PIZZA
Basic Mother Dough (page 55)
Pizza slice (yellow: Turmeric, page 56; or orange: Harissa, page 61)
Pepperoni (red: Beet-Paprika, page 63)
Crust (brown: Cacao, page 46; or orange: Harissa, page 61, as shown)

So to make these four emojis for an emoji party, here are the dough colors needed:

Basic Mother Dough
Beet-Paprika
Turmeric
Cacao
Activated Charcoal
Milk
Butterfly Pea Flower or Spirulina
Harissa

When you've decided which emojis to make and which colors you'll need to make them, prepare the dough. You can make half batches of everything but the Basic Mother Dough (page 55) if all you're making are emojis, or you can go ahead and make full batches and sheet out any remaining dough for noodles to be eaten at your leisure.

HEART EMOJI RAVIOLONI

1. Start with a base pasta sheet that is rolled to the second-thinnest setting on your pasta machine. You'll need a top and bottom sheet, and both sheets should be 5- to 6-inch squares, though larger won't hurt anything, and that way you'll have plenty of room to cut them down to whatever size you wish.

2. Roll out a quarter-size piece of the beet-paprika dough to the second-thinnest setting on a pasta machine.

3. Use a 2- to 3-inch heart cutter to cut a heart shape out of the red pasta. Alternatively, you can trace and cut out a heart onto a sheet of parchment paper, then attach the parchment heart to the red sheet with a tiny droplet of water. You can use clean scissors to cut the

heart shape out, quickly removing the parchment so it doesn't permanently stick to the heart.

4. Paint a small amount of water onto the center of one of the base sheets and press the heart onto the center of the base sheet.

5. If you would like your heart to have more definition, you can outline it with a thin strand of red pasta either made with the spaghetti cutter attachment for the pasta machine, or sliced thin using a straight rolling pasta cutter. To adhere the strand, paint a small amount of water onto the outermost edge of the red heart and attach the thin strand to the edge of the heart, not the base sheet around the heart. Use scissors to cut any excess strand after you've fully outlined the heart. Do not attach the strand to the base sheet, or you may notice a gap between the outline and the heart when the pasta dries.

6. Wipe away any excess water from the design using a dry paintbrush. Use a

rolling pin to gently seal the heart to the base sheet, by rolling gently back and forth in all directions so you don't skew the design too much in any one direction.

7. Follow the instructions for filling the emoji ravioloni on page 167.

LAUGH-CRY EMOJI RAVIOLONI

1. Start with a base pasta sheet that is rolled to the second-thinnest setting on your pasta machine. You'll need a top and bottom sheet, and both sheets should be 5- to 6-inch squares, though larger won't hurt anything, and that way you'll have plenty of room to cut them down to whatever size you wish.

2. Roll out a quarter-size piece of the turmeric dough to the second-thinnest setting on a pasta machine.

3. Use a 2½-inch round cutter to cut out a yellow circle.

4. Paint a small amount of water onto the center of one of the base sheets and press the yellow circle "face" onto the center of the base sheet. Use a rolling pin to gently affix it to the base sheet.

5. Roll out a quarter-size piece of the cacao dough to the second-thinnest setting on a pasta machine (some people prefer black, not brown, so

use the charcoal dough instead if you wish). Cut it into thin strands using the spaghetti cutter on your pasta machine, or freehand with a straight rolling cutter. Paint a line of water around the perimeter of the yellow face circle just on the edge of the yellow, not on the base sheet or the outline of the emoji will separate from the actual face.

mouth. Paint a small line of water where the teeth should go on the yellow circle and place the teeth on the prepped area using tweezers or your fingers. Paint around the teeth where the mouth should be with a small amount of water. Use a long strand of the brown dough to outline the teeth and form the mouth.

10. Roll out a dime-size piece of the blue (butterfly pea or spirulina) dough. Cut two teardrop shapes out of it that are about ¾ inch long. You can do this in several ways: Use a fondant cutter to make petals, then cut the petals into teardrops with a straight rolling cutter. Freehand teardrop shapes using a straight rolling cutter. Trace a teardrop onto parchment, cut out the parchment teardrop, and use it as a template to cut out uniform pasta teardrops.

6. Outline the yellow circle face with a strand of the cacao dough, again keeping it on the yellow face, not on the base sheet, to avoid separation between the outline and the face.

7. Cut the cacao strand into four ½-inch pieces for the eyes and eyebrows. Paint a small line of water on the yellow circle where the eyes and eyebrows should go, and place the four lines on the prepped area using either your fingers or tweezers. Tweezers may help you to get the angle of the lines just right.

8. Roll out a dime-size piece of the milk dough to the second-thinnest setting on a pasta machine.

9. Use a 2¼-inch round cutter to cut a small crescent shape out of the side of the white sheet. This should look like the teeth on the inside of the laughing

11. Paint a small dab of water where the teardrops should go on both the yellow face and just off it onto the base sheet. Press the teardrops in place.

12. Wipe away any excess water from the design using a dry paintbrush. Use a rolling pin to gently seal the design to the base sheet, by rolling gently back and forth in all directions so you don't skew the design too much in any one direction.

13. Follow the instructions for filling the emoji ravioloni on page 167.

POOP EMOJI RAVIOLONI

1. Start with a base pasta sheet that is rolled to the second-thinnest setting on your pasta machine. You'll need a top and bottom sheet, and both sheets should be 5- to 6-inch squares, though larger won't hurt anything, and that way you'll have plenty of room to cut them down to whatever size you wish.

2. Roll out a quarter-size piece of the cacao dough to the second-thinnest setting on a pasta machine. Cut out a poop emoji shape by using either a 2- or 3-inch poop emoji cutter or the parchment template method. To make a parchment paper template, pull up a picture of the poop emoji on your computer or phone, or refer to a hard copy. Size it to about 2½ inches tall and trace it onto parchment paper. Cut out the shape and affix the parchment to the cacao sheet with a dab of water. Use clean kitchen scissors to cut the pasta following the parchment template, then remove the parchment.

3. Paint a small amount of water onto the center of one of the base sheets and press the design onto the center of the base sheet. Use a rolling pin to gently affix it to the base sheet.

4. Roll out a quarter-size piece of the milk dough and a dime-size piece of the charcoal dough to the second-thinnest setting on a pasta machine. Cut out round eyeballs about ½ inch in diameter using a round cutter or large piping tip. Use your fingers to stretch them into ovals. Paint a small amount of water onto the poop design where the eyeballs go and affix the eyeballs.

5. Cut out round pupils about ³⁄₁₆ inch in diameter using the black pasta sheet and a small piping tip or round cutter. Paint a small amount of water onto the eyeballs where the pupils go and affix the pupils.

6. Use a 2¼-inch round cutter to cut a small crescent shape out of the side of the white sheet. This should look like a smiling mouth. Paint a small amount of water onto the poop design where the mouth should go and affix the mouth.

7. Use a dry paintbrush to wipe away any excess water from the design. Use a rolling pin to gently seal the design to the base sheet, rolling gently back and forth in all directions so you don't skew the design too much in any one direction.

8. Follow the instructions for filling the emoji ravioloni on the opposite page.

PIZZA EMOJI RAVIOLONI

1. Start with a base pasta sheet that is rolled to the second-thinnest setting on your pasta machine. You'll need a top and bottom sheet, and both sheets should be 5- to 6-inch squares, though larger won't hurt anything, and that way you'll have plenty of room to cut them down to whatever size you wish.

2. Roll out a quarter-size piece of the turmeric dough to the second-thinnest setting on a pasta machine. Use a straight rolling cutter to cut a slice-shaped triangle out of the yellow sheet that is 2½ inches tall. Make the "crust" edge slightly rounded, as on a pizza slice.

3. Paint a small amount of water onto the center of one of the base sheets and

press the design onto the center of the base sheet. Use a rolling pin to gently affix it to the base sheet.

4. Roll out a dime-size piece of beet-paprika dough to the second-thinnest setting on a pasta machine. Cut five pieces of "pepperoni" out of it using a piping tip or small round cutter with a ¼-inch tip. Cut one of the pepperoni circles in half to form the sliced pepperoni at the bottom of the pepperoni emoji. Paint a small amount of water where each of the pepperoni pieces goes on the slice and affix them to the slice using tweezers or your fingers.

5. Roll out a dime-size piece of the harissa dough to the second-thinnest setting on a pasta machine. Cut it into a thin strand using the spaghetti cutter on the pasta machine or a straight rolling cutter. Paint a small amount of water in an oval shape at the top (rounded) part of the pizza slice. Place the harissa strand at the top of the pizza slice in an oval shape, leaving a little bit of yellow exposed in the middle of the oval to represent the puffy, less "done" part of the crust.

6. Use a dry paintbrush to wipe away any excess water from the design. Use a rolling pin to gently seal the design to the base sheet, rolling gently back and forth in all directions so you don't skew the design too much in any one direction.

7. Follow the instructions for filling the emoji ravioloni here.

HOW TO FILL RAVIOLONI

1. Uncover the reserved bottom sheet of pasta and use your fingers to dab a small circle of flour in the middle of the sheet where you'll place the filling. This helps keep the pasta touching the filling from getting soggy. Place about ¼ cup of your chosen filling (or 1 burrata ball) on the flour circle. Use a brush to paint the base sheet with water around the filling so that the top sheet will adhere to it. Pick up your emoji top sheet and align it over the base sheet, pattern side up. Very gently set the top sheet over the filling, taking care to push air bubbles to the edges and avoid wrinkling the top sheet.

2. The blunt side (*not the sharp side*) of a round cookie cutter will work very well here to smooth all the bubbles and flatten the top sheet to the base sheet. Just roll the upside-down cutter in a gentle, circular motion around the filling until the pasta is smooth and there is a nice, defined line between the flat part of the raviolone and the filling.

3. You do not technically have to cut these ravioloni to crimp them, but you may if you wish. You can keep them as squares, or even turn your cookie cutter over and cut them into circles. Bear in mind that the more pasta you leave on the ravioloni, the more you'll get to eat later. I prefer 4½-inch flute-edged squares.

4. Repeat to fill the remaining ravioloni.

5. Store the ravioloni uncovered on parchment-lined and semolina-dusted sheet pans. They can be kept at room temperature for up to 2 hours or in the refrigerator uncovered for up to 6 hours.

6. Use as large a stockpot as you can for these and boil 2 or 3 at a time in salted water for 4 minutes. Drain, dress, and serve immediately.

FREEHAND PASTA ART: THE LONG AND SHORT OF IT

If you've read this far and made some of the pasta and patterns up to this point, you've probably figured out that pasta itself can become not only your canvas, but also your brush and ink. I hope I've given you some novel pattern ideas in this chapter, but I would be remiss if I didn't also encourage you to run with your own imagination. I wake up most mornings with a brain full of inspiration, and I can't wait to get to my pasta board so I can translate those ephemeral ideas into sweeping gestures. If you can dream it, by and large, you can put it on a sheet of pasta. By now I hope you have the mechanics of making mountains with matcha dough, and here are some tips that might help you refine your technique.

Think about pasta like cake or cookie decorating and your perspective will totally change. Many of those same tools you've seen master cake artists use have applications in pasta art as well. Sharp, tiny scissors are ideal for cutting excess strands of pasta you've used to draw lines with. Tweezers can help you lay lines, dots, eyeballs, tears, or other tiny shapes when your hands are a bit too ungainly to do the job. Plunger cutters can make quick work of shaped cutouts. I love to walk through cake-decorating stores,

spaghetti-thickness noodles, you'll wind up with thin, delicate strokes, whereas if you use fettuccine- or pappardelle-thickness noodles, your lines will be bolder. Conjure a picture you want to paint onto pasta, whether it's an homage to your favorite celebrity, a landscape, or even a pasta replica of a piece of fine art, and study the lines. Match them with the thickness of your noodles and start small but think big.

Since pasta dries so quickly, be sure to cover any areas you've already worked on, and sheet out only a little bit of dough at a time so that it doesn't dry out and go to waste. Any pasta you're using to make lines or designs will dry even faster because it's already cut into tiny pieces. In general, I tend to work with quarter-size pieces of dough or smaller.

Mostly I'd like to encourage you to tap in to your own creative genius. I'd love for this book to launch you talented readers on your own quest to create beautiful things—and I'd also really love to see them. If you have any questions about tools, tips, tricks, dough, and the like, or if you want to share with me the beautiful things you've created, you're always welcome to contact me through social media or e-mail.

stare at the tools, and get ideas. I do this in the hardware store too, but that's another story.

When you're making designs using pasta as your pen and ink, consider the boldness of your line. If you use

4

GNOCCHI AND OTHER ROLLED PASTA

Gnocchi, gnudi, and gnocchetti are not pasta shapes in the pure sense. Rather, they are dumplings made with flour, sometimes eggs, potatoes, or ricotta, and in the case of the recipes in this book, a colorful flavor ingredient. You don't need a pasta machine to make gnocchi. You need little more than your hands and a good feel for the dough consistency. Because of this, I think of them as the predecessors of pasta, and certainly the best place to start if you don't own a bunch of fancy gadgets but still want to try your floury hand at pasta making.

When you are rolling out gnocchi, it is helpful to get a feel for the right moisture level of the dough. If it's coated in too much flour, it won't roll out into long, even snakes. Instead it will blob up in places and potentially rip and tear in others. On the other hand, if the dough is too gloppy, it will stick to the work surface and make a mess. You'll learn just the right feel as you practice more. It's better to err on the side of too much flour. I like to keep a damp paper towel nearby and wipe my hands on it periodically to provide just enough grip that the dough rolls out evenly.

Please resist the urge to boil the beets or sweet potatoes called for in the gnocchi recipes that follow. Tubers meant for gnocchi must be dry-cooked: baked or microwaved. And while we're on the subject, there is no standard potato gnocchi recipe in this book, but if you ever do make it, be mindful that boiling potatoes before gnocchi-fying them will yield tough, waterlogged dumplings fit for the compost pile, not your composed palate.

CHOOSING YOUR RICOTTA

Most of these rolled dough recipes call for drained whole milk ricotta, because it gives gnocchi its signature pillowy quality. Please do not be tempted to use skim milk ricotta in place of whole milk ricotta. Its runny texture will make the gnocchi dense and drown your downy dreams. If you're looking for a producer recommendation, Bellwether

Farms churns out hand-dipped Jersey cow milk ricotta that's sold in its original draining basket (a draining basket is a good sign in general). The curds are soft and ultra-creamy, not gritty, thin, or grainy like some supermarket ricotta can be. Calabro is a slightly larger producer that also makes excellent fresh-tasting, sweet cream ricotta. Calabro has a higher moisture content than Bellwether, so don't skimp on the draining step outlined in each recipe. Homemade ricotta is also an easy-to-make, excellent option, if you have the time and inclination.

FUN WITH ROLLING GNOCCHI

Play around with your silicone sushi mat or gnocchi board. You can run rolled dough straight across it or at a diagonal, and even play with which side of each gnocco hits the grooves first. If you roll the cut side of the gnocco against the mat, it will be more football shaped, whereas if you roll the smooth, outer side that has more flour on it against the mat, the batch of gnocchi will look kind of like those big round hay bales in farm fields that dot the sides of country roads.

If you don't have a silicone sushi mat or a gnocchi board, you can also roll against a cheese grater, the tines of a fork, a colander, or any sort of textured

doohickey you may happen upon, as long as it's clean and food-safe.

COOKING GNOCCHI

You can test the level of doneness of gnocchi by removing one from the water with a slotted spoon and cutting it in half. If it looks (and tastes) cooked through, the remaining gnocchi are ready to emerge from the water like voluptuous Venuses.

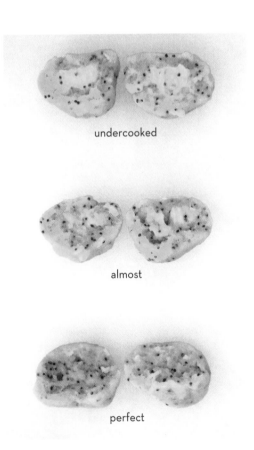

undercooked

almost

perfect

BEET GNOCCHI

These gnocchi are delightfully rustic compared with the rest of the often, shall we say, "precious" recipes in this book. No special equipment is needed beyond a vegetable peeler, box grater, and knife or bench scraper. The gnocchi are left deliberately ungrooved, because their texture is rough enough to encourage the slipperiest of sauces to hang on.

These gnocchi love to be bathed in the Bacon-Peanut-Tomato Sauce on page 213.

MAKES 4 SERVINGS

1 medium red beet
One 15-ounce tub whole milk ricotta cheese, drained in cheesecloth
    for 15 minutes
½ cup freshly grated Parmigiano-Reggiano cheese
1 large egg
½ teaspoon freshly grated nutmeg
1 teaspoon kosher salt, or more as needed
1¾ cups "00" pasta flour, plus more for dusting
1 tablespoon butter (use bacon fat if you're serving with the Bacon-
    Peanut-Tomato Sauce)
1 tablespoon olive oil

1. Wrap the beet in a damp paper towel and microwave it on high for 5 minutes. It will not be completely soft; don't be alarmed. When the beet is cool enough to handle, peel it and grate it on the medium holes of a box grater into a medium bowl.

2. Add the ricotta, Parmigiano, egg, nutmeg, and salt and stir to thoroughly combine. Stir in 1 cup of the flour until completely mixed. Add the remaining flour a little at a time, pulling the dough away from the sides of the bowl.

3. When the dough is no longer tacky, turn it out onto a floured surface and knead gently into a ball, adding flour as needed to keep the dough from sticking to the surface. Knead for about 2 minutes, until the dough is uniform. Do not overknead or the gnocchi will be tough.

4. Cut the dough into four pieces and roll each into a snake that is ⅔ inch in diameter. When you're rolling the snakes, keep in mind that they will roll more uniformly if you can use as little flour as possible, but you'll want to roll quickly

back and forth so that the snakes don't stick to the surface.

5. Line the snakes up next to one another and flour them so they don't stick together. Using a pastry cutter, cut the snakes into ½-inch pieces. Roll a gnocco between the palms of your hands until it's rounded, and repeat with the remaining gnocchi. Toss the gnocchi in flour.

6. Line a sheet pan with parchment paper and lightly dust it with flour. Arrange the gnocchi on the pan and refrigerate, uncovered, for at least 30 minutes or up to 2 hours.

7. Preheat the oven to 425°F and bring a large pot of salted water to a boil.

Working in batches of fifteen or so at a time, boil the gnocchi until they float to the top of the pot, 1 to 3 minutes. Test the gnocchi for doneness by removing one with a slotted spoon and cutting it in half. If it looks (and tastes) cooked through, the batch is ready to be removed. If it is gooey, continue boiling and retest.

8. Meanwhile, put the butter and oil in a 9 by 13-inch baking dish.

9. Remove the gnocchi from the water with a slotted spoon or spider and put them in the baking dish. Repeat to cook the rest of the gnocchi. Stir to coat well with the butter and oil, then bake for 10 minutes, gently stirring once after 5 minutes. Sauce and serve immediately.

BURRATA GNOCCHI

What started as a happy accident—I had a glut of burrata and needed to use it fast—became one of my most beloved recipes (and the one most requested by friends and family). You may not think it's worth dismembering glistening balls of burrata, but I'd urge you to close your eyes and imagine its heavenly, pillowy texture, and then picture that same ethereal lightness in tiny pasta dumpling form. Intrigued? Get cooking, then, because you're in for a treat.

In Italy, burrata can come in different sizes, but here in the States, most burrata is formed into 4-ounce balls. A standard 8-ounce container will include two 4-ounce balls, and this recipe calls for four balls of burrata—in other words, two containers will have you on your way to this pasta paradise. BelGioioso is a common brand to look for in well-stocked grocery stores, and Trader Joe's also sells burrata made by a Wisconsin cheesemaker. Be sure to look for as distant an expiration date as you can—burrata spoils fast.

Burrata gnocchi's soul mate is the roasted tomatoes with basil oil sauce on page 214, but as you can guess, there is no need to finish the sauce with extra burrata, since it's already in the gnocchi. MAKES 4 SERVINGS

> Four 4-ounce balls of burrata cheese (two 8-ounce containers),
>   drained and patted dry with paper towels
> ½ cup freshly grated Parmigiano-Reggiano cheese
> 1 large egg
> ¼ teaspoon freshly grated nutmeg
> 1¾ cups "00" pasta flour, plus more for dusting
> Kosher salt
> 1 tablespoon butter
> 1 tablespoon olive oil

1. Pulse the burrata, Parmigiano, egg, and nutmeg in a food processor until just combined, about 10 seconds.

2. In a medium bowl, combine the puree and 1 cup of the flour and stir until combined. Add the remaining flour a little at a time, pulling the dough away from the sides of the bowl.

3. When the dough is no longer tacky, turn it out onto a floured surface and knead gently into a ball, adding flour as needed to keep the dough from sticking to the surface. Knead for about 2 minutes, until the dough is uniform. Do not overknead or the gnocchi will be tough.

4. Cut the dough into four pieces and roll each piece into a snake that is ⅔ inch in diameter. When you're rolling the snakes, keep in mind that they will roll more uniformly if you can use as little flour as possible, but you'll want to roll quickly back and forth so that the snakes don't stick to the surface.

5. Line the snakes up next to one another and flour them so they don't stick together. Using a pastry cutter, cut the snakes into ½-inch pieces. Toss the gnocchi in flour.

6. If you would like grooves in your gnocchi, place either a silicone sushi mat or a gnocchi board in front of you with the grooves running perpendicular to the edge of the counter closest to you. Set a gnocco parallel to the counter on the board or mat and use your thumb to roll it against the board or mat, pushing the grooves away from you. Press firmly enough to imprint grooves but gently enough that you don't squish the shape. Repeat to imprint the entire batch.

7. Line a sheet pan with parchment paper and lightly dust it with flour. Arrange the gnocchi on the sheet pan. Refrigerate, uncovered, for at least 30 minutes or up to 2 hours.

8. Preheat the oven to 425°F and bring a large pot of salted water to boil. Working in batches of fifteen or so at a time, boil the gnocchi until they float to the top of the pot, 1 to 3 minutes. Test the gnocchi for doneness by removing one with a slotted spoon and cutting it in half. If it looks (and tastes) cooked through, the batch is ready to remove. If it is gooey, continue boiling and retest.

9. Meanwhile, put the butter and oil in a 9 by 13-inch baking dish.

10. Remove the gnocchi from the water with a slotted spoon or spider and put them in the baking dish. Repeat to cook the rest of the gnocchi. Stir to coat well with the butter and oil, then bake for 10 minutes, gently stirring once after 5 minutes. Sauce and serve immediately.

MINT PEA GNOCCHI

Peas and mint are one of life's perfect combinations. There is archaeological evidence to suggest that people were eating peas eight thousand years ago, and mint has been found in Egyptian tombs dating back to 1000 B.C. So my question to you, dear readers, is which lucky individual first tasted mint and peas together? These are the arcane questions that make me want to travel backward in time.

Bathe these gnocchi in either Lemon Cream Sauce (page 228) or Spiced Lamb Yogurt Sauce (page 246).

MAKES 4 VERY GENEROUS MAIN-COURSE SERVINGS OR 6 FIRST-COURSE SERVINGS

1 teaspoon kosher salt, or more as needed
¼ teaspoon baking soda
6 ounces frozen peas (1 cup)
1½ cups packed fresh mint leaves (about 1 ounce)
2 large eggs
12 ounces whole milk ricotta cheese (about 1⅓ cups), drained in cheesecloth for 15 minutes
⅔ cup freshly grated Parmigiano-Reggiano cheese
½ teaspoon freshly grated nutmeg
1¾ cups "00" pasta flour, plus more for dusting
1 tablespoon butter
1 tablespoon olive oil

1. Bring 4 cups water to a boil in a medium saucepan along with the salt and baking soda. Blanch the peas and mint for 5 seconds, then immediately drain in a strainer. Let the peas cool in the strainer for 2 minutes, then gently press out any remaining water.

2. Puree the peas, mint, and eggs in a blender until smooth. In a medium bowl, combine the puree, ricotta, Parmigiano, and nutmeg and stir until thoroughly combined. Add 1 cup of the flour and stir until a ball of dough forms. Add the remaining flour a little at a time, pulling the dough away from the sides of the bowl.

3. When the dough is no longer tacky, turn it out onto a floured surface and knead gently into a ball, adding flour as needed to keep the dough from sticking to the surface. Knead for about 2 minutes, until the dough is uniform. Do not overknead or the gnocchi will be tough.

4. Cut the dough into eight pieces and roll each piece into a snake that is ⅔ inch in diameter. When you're rolling the snakes, keep in mind that they will roll more uniformly if you can use as little flour as possible, but you'll want to roll quickly back and forth so that the snakes don't stick to the surface.

5. Line four snakes up next to one another and flour them so they don't stick together. Using a pastry cutter, cut

the snakes into ½-inch pieces. Repeat with the remaining four snakes. Toss the gnocchi in flour.

6. If you would like grooves in your gnocchi, place either a silicone sushi mat or a gnocchi board in front of you with the grooves running perpendicular to the edge of the counter closest to you. Set a gnocco parallel to the counter on the board or mat and use your thumb to roll it against the board or mat, pushing the grooves away from you. Press firmly enough to imprint grooves but gently enough that you don't squish the shape. Repeat to imprint the entire batch.

7. Line a sheet pan (or two) with parchment paper and lightly dust it with flour. Arrange the gnocchi on the sheet pan so that they are not touching. Refrigerate, uncovered, for at least 30 minutes or up to 2 hours.

8. Preheat the oven to 425°F and bring a large pot of salted water to a boil. Working in batches of fifteen or so at a time, boil the gnocchi until they float to the top of the pot, 1 to 3 minutes. Test the gnocchi for doneness by removing one with a slotted spoon and cutting it in half. If it looks (and tastes) cooked through, they are done.

9. Meanwhile, put the butter and oil in a 9 by 13-inch baking dish.

10. Remove the gnocchi from the water with a slotted spoon or spider and put them in the baking dish. Repeat to cook the rest of the gnocchi. Stir to coat well with the butter and oil, then bake for 10 minutes, gently stirring once after 5 minutes. Sauce and serve immediately.

PURPLE SWEET POTATO GNOCCHI

This recipe will work with any sweet potato, but if you buy purple-fleshed sweet potatoes, your gnocchi will be this spectacularly regal shade. Look for a grower called Frieda's and a variety called Stokes Purple. You can see where their potatoes are available by state by looking at the store locator on www.friedas.com, or you can order them online. Aside from the deep, vibrant color, the texture is drier than most sweet potatoes, which makes for perfect gnocchi texture.

Note that these sweet potatoes are not Okinawan sweet potatoes or Ube, which yield gnocchi in a much lighter, grayish-tinged color.

Cover these gnocchi in Walnut and Poppy Seed Browned Butter (page 205).

MAKES 4 SERVINGS

1½ pounds Stokes Purple sweet potato (generally 1 large or 2 small)
1 cup whole milk ricotta cheese, drained in cheesecloth for 15 minutes
1 loosely packed cup freshly grated Parmigiano-Reggiano cheese
1½ teaspoons kosher salt, or more as needed
1 teaspoon garam masala (optional)
1¼ cups "00" pasta flour, plus more for dusting
1 tablespoon butter
1 tablespoon olive oil

1. Wrap the sweet potato(es) in a damp paper towel and microwave until soft, 4 to 6 minutes, depending on your microwave. Let cool enough to handle (remember, it's called hot potato for a reason), and peel as best as you can. Pass it into a large bowl through a food mill or potato ricer, or in a pinch, grate it on the large holes of a box grater. You'll have about 3 loosely packed cups potato, but don't get too fussy about measuring; this recipe is forgiving in either direction.

2. Add the ricotta, Parmigiano, salt, and garam masala (if using) to the bowl and stir to combine. Add 1 cup of the flour and stir until a ball of dough forms. Add the remaining flour a little at a time, pulling the dough away from the sides of the bowl.

3. When the dough is no longer tacky, turn it out onto a floured surface and knead gently into a ball, adding flour as needed to keep the dough from sticking to the surface. Knead for about

2 minutes, until the dough is uniform. Do not overknead or the gnocchi will be tough.

4. Cut the dough into eight pieces and roll each piece into a snake that is ⅔ inch in diameter. When you're rolling the snakes, keep in mind that they will roll more uniformly if you can use as little flour as possible, but you'll want to roll quickly back and forth so that the snakes don't stick to the surface.

5. Line four snakes up next to one another and flour them so they don't stick together. Using a pastry cutter, cut the snakes into ½-inch pieces. Repeat with the remaining four snakes. Toss the gnocchi in flour.

6. If you would like grooves in your gnocchi, place either a silicone sushi mat or a gnocchi board in front of you with the grooves running perpendicular to the edge of the counter closest to you.

Set a gnocco parallel to the counter on the mat or board and use your thumb to roll it against the mat or board, pushing the grooves away from you. Press firmly enough to imprint grooves but gently enough that you don't squish the shape. Repeat to imprint the entire batch.

7. Line a sheet pan (or two) with parchment paper and lightly dust it with flour. Arrange the gnocchi on the sheet pan so that they are not touching. Refrigerate, uncovered, for at least 30 minutes or up to 2 hours.

8. Preheat the oven to 425°F and bring a large pot of salted water to boil. Working in batches of fifteen or so at a time, boil the gnocchi until they float to the top of the pot, 1 to 3 minutes. Test the gnocchi for doneness by removing one with a slotted spoon and cutting it in half. If it looks (and tastes) cooked through, they are done.

9. Meanwhile, put the butter and oil in a 9 by 13-inch baking dish.

10. Remove the gnocchi from the water with a slotted spoon or spider and put them in the baking dish. Repeat to cook the rest of the gnocchi. Stir to coat well with the butter and oil, then bake for 10 minutes, gently stirring once after 5 minutes. Sauce and serve immediately.

AVOCADO GNOCCHI

This recipe came about as a fluke-gone-good. I've turned nearly everything under the sun into pasta, but somehow avocado escaped my floury clutches until one day I spied an avocado on the counter next to an open container of ricotta—and an idea was born. I didn't actually think it would work, I have to admit, and I figured that even if I got the texture right, it would surely brown before it hit the plate. Boy, was I ever wrong. Avocado lovers go ape over this gnocchi, because the avocado flavor really comes through. I would say it's probably not a recipe for the avocado-wary, but then, I can't remember the last time I met someone who didn't like avocado.

Please be sure to use an avocado that is ripe enough for you to mash but not one that has brown spots inside, as the brown will make its way into the gnocchi and no one wants that.

Serve these gnocchi with either Lemon Cream Sauce (page 228) or Paprika Browned Butter (page 204). MAKES 4 SERVINGS

1 large, ripe avocado (but no brown spots or streaks inside!)
1 tablespoon freshly squeezed lemon juice
1 cup whole milk ricotta cheese, drained in cheesecloth for 15 minutes
1 large egg
1 teaspoon kosher salt, or more as needed
1/2 cup freshly grated Parmigiano-Reggiano cheese
1¾ cups "00" pasta flour, plus more for dusting
1 tablespoon butter
1 tablespoon olive oil

1. In a medium bowl, mash the avocado and lemon juice together with a silicone spatula until smooth. Add the ricotta, egg, salt, and Parmigiano and stir until well combined. Add 1 cup of the flour and stir until a ball of dough forms. Add the remaining flour a little at a time, pulling the dough away from the sides of the bowl.

2. When the dough is no longer tacky, turn it out onto a floured surface and knead gently into a ball, adding flour as needed to keep the dough from sticking to the surface. Knead for about 2 minutes, until the dough is uniform. Do not overknead or the gnocchi will be tough.

3. Cut the dough into four pieces and roll each piece into a snake that is ⅔ inch in diameter. When you're rolling the snakes, keep in mind that they will roll more uniformly if you can use as little flour as possible, but you'll want to roll quickly back and forth so that the snakes don't stick to the surface.

4. Line the snakes up next to one another and flour them so they don't stick together. Using a pastry cutter, cut the snakes into ½-inch pieces. Toss the gnocchi in flour.

5. If you would like grooves in your gnocchi, place either a silicone sushi mat or a gnocchi board in front of you with the grooves running perpendicular to the edge of the counter closest to you. Set a gnocco parallel to the counter on the board or mat and use your thumb to roll it against the board or mat, pushing the grooves away from you. Press firmly enough to imprint grooves but gently enough that you don't squish the shape. Repeat to imprint the entire batch.

6. Line a sheet pan with parchment paper and lightly dust it with flour. Arrange the gnocchi on the sheet pan and cover it with plastic wrap. Refrigerate for at least 30 minutes or up to 2 hours. Any longer and the gnocchi may brown.

7. Preheat the oven to 425°F and bring a large pot of salted water to a boil. Working in batches of fifteen or so at a time, boil the gnocchi until they float to the top of the pot, about 1 to 3 minutes. Test the gnocchi for doneness by removing one with a slotted spoon and cutting it in half. If it looks (and tastes) cooked through, they are done.

8. Meanwhile, put the butter and oil in a 9 by 13-inch baking dish.

9. Remove the gnocchi from the water with a slotted spoon or spider and place them in the baking dish. Repeat to cook the rest of the gnocchi. Stir to coat well with the butter and oil, then bake for 10 minutes, gently stirring once after 5 minutes. Sauce and serve immediately.

BEET RICOTTA GNUDI

Gnudi are what happens when gnocchi and big, German dumplings have babies. Fluffy, airy, cheesy babies that you love to eat, so maybe we should ditch the baby metaphor now, because nobody eats babies. Except maybe dingoes. In any case, gnudi are your new best friends, so make them for a crowd, or even a romantic feast for two. Might I suggest Valentine's Day?

Don't be tempted to cook the beet any other way than specified in this recipe. Moisture is the enemy of good gnudi, and boiling, steaming, or otherwise cooking the beet with water will not only throw off the delicate moisture balance here, it will also diminish the gorgeous color the beet imparts.

The gnudi are flavorful enough to serve as is, with just a bit of Parmigiano-Reggiano grated over the top, but they're also lovely in Butternut Squash and Goat Cheese Sauce with Pine Nuts (page 227). MAKES 4 SERVINGS

1 medium red beet, peeled and roughly chopped
2 large eggs
One 15-ounce tub whole milk ricotta cheese, drained in cheesecloth
    for 15 minutes
2/3 cup freshly grated Parmigiano-Reggiano cheese, plus more for
    serving, as desired
2 tablespoons butter, melted and cooled slightly, plus 1½ tablespoons
    for the sauté pan
¼ teaspoon freshly grated nutmeg
1½ cups "00" pasta flour, or more as needed
¼ cup poppy seeds (optional)
Kosher salt
1 tablespoon olive oil

1. Put the beet in a small, non-metal bowl and cover with plastic wrap. Microwave for 50 seconds. Let sit for 2 minutes. Combine the beet and eggs in a blender and blend on low speed, slowly increasing speed until a smooth puree forms.

2. In a medium bowl, mix the puree, ricotta, Parmigiano, melted butter, and nutmeg with a rubber spatula until uniform. Slowly fold in the flour and poppy seeds (if using), just until the mixture pulls away from the sides of the bowl. Do not overmix or add too much

flour or your gnudi will be tough. Sprinkle flour over the mixture until the outsides are all coated and not sticking to the bowl.

3. Line a sheet pan with parchment paper and flour the parchment generously. Flour your hands and gently tear off a 1-inch chunk of dough (or you can use a small scoop to portion out your chunks more evenly). Roll the dough between your floured palms just until a ball forms; it should be nearly the size of a Ping-Pong ball. Do not over-roll or you'll wind up with tough gnudi. Place the dough ball on the sheet pan and repeat to roll the rest of the dough. Strive for uniformity in size. If some are bigger or smaller, you will wind up with some that are mushy and overcooked and some that are liquidy inside.

4. Cover the sheet pan and refrigerate immediately for at least 30 minutes so they have a chance to firm up. This pasta does not store well, so I recommend cooking within 3 hours.

5. Bring a generous amount of salted water to a boil in a large pot over high heat and, in a large sauté pan over medium heat, heat the oil and the remaining 1½ tablespoons butter.

6. Boil half of the gnudi until they float, 3 to 5 minutes. Gently stir the gnudi occasionally with a wooden spoon to keep them from sticking to the bottom of the pot. Test the gnudi for doneness by removing one with a slotted spoon and cutting it in half. If it looks (and tastes) cooked through, they are done. Repeat with the remaining gnudi.

7. Gently remove the gnudi with a large slotted spoon or spider and brown them in the sauté pan until slightly firm on all sides, about 4 minutes. You may have to do this in batches if your sauté pan is not large enough. Toss with sauce or cheese and serve immediately.

ESPRESSO CHESTNUT GNOCCHETTI

These gnocchetti are the autumn food you wind up craving all year. They are somewhat smaller than classic gnocchi and contain no potato. They love to bathe in cheesy cream sauces and have enough flavor themselves that it would be a shame to smother them beneath something too spicy or complicated. I love them with Piemontese Cheese Sauce (page 231). The espresso is a surprising and delightful addition if you're a coffee lover, but even if you're not, give it a go. It enhances the flavor of the chestnut in much the same way that it can heighten chocolate in baking recipes. You may substitute unsweetened black cold-brewed coffee for espresso if you wish, although the flavor will be slightly less pronounced. MAKES 4 SERVINGS

1¾ cups "00" pasta flour, plus more for dusting
⅓ cup chestnut flour
¼ cup brewed espresso, slightly cooled
1 large egg
1 cup whole milk ricotta, drained in cheesecloth for 15 minutes
Kosher salt
1 tablespoon butter
1 tablespoon olive oil

1. Add both flours to a medium bowl and stir to combine. In a small bowl, lightly whisk the espresso and egg together. Make a well in the center of the flour and add the ricotta. Pour the espresso mixture over the ricotta. Stir with a silicone spatula until the mixture comes together into a rough dough.

2. Lightly flour your work surface and turn the dough out onto it. Knead the dough just until it is uniform; overkneading will result in tough gnocchetti. Cover the ball of dough with plastic wrap and let it rest for 30 minutes.

3. Uncover the dough and divide it into four pieces, using a bench scraper. Roll each piece into a snake that is ½ inch in diameter. Line the snakes up next to one another and flour them so they don't stick together. Using a pastry cutter, cut the snakes into ¼-inch pieces. Toss the gnocchetti in flour.

4. If you would like grooves in your gnocchetti, place either a silicone sushi mat or a gnocchi board in front of you with the grooves running perpendicular to the edge of the counter closest to you. Set a gnocchetto parallel to the

counter on the board or mat and use your thumb to roll it against the board or mat, pushing the grooves away from you. Press firmly enough to imprint grooves but gently enough that you don't squish the shape. Repeat to imprint the entire batch.

5. Line a sheet pan with parchment paper and lightly dust it with flour. Arrange the gnocchetti on the sheet pan and cover it with plastic wrap. Refrigerate for at least 30 minutes or up to 6 hours.

6. Preheat the oven to 425°F and bring a pot of salted water to a boil. Working in batches of fifteen or so at a time, boil the gnocchetti until they float to the top of the pot, 1 to 3 minutes. Test the gnocchetti for doneness by removing one with a slotted spoon and cutting it in half. If it looks (and tastes) cooked through, they are done.

7. Meanwhile, put the butter and oil in a 9 by 13-inch baking dish.

8. Remove the gnocchetti from the water with a slotted spoon or spider and put them in the baking dish. Repeat to cook the rest of the gnocchetti. Stir to coat well with the butter and oil, then bake for 10 minutes, gently stirring once after 5 minutes. Sauce and serve immediately.

TURMERIC-POPPY SEED-RICOTTA GNUDI

The bright-yellow interior of these gnudi offers a stark contrast to the poppy seed speckles, so even though I list them as optional, I think of them as essential to the vibe of the dish. I also flat-out love the Pop Rocks surprise crunch quality they lend to the otherwise pillowy gnudi.

The gnudi are flavorful enough to serve as is, with just a bit of Parmigiano-Reggiano grated over the top, but they're also lovely in Butternut Squash and Goat Cheese Sauce with Pine Nuts (page 227). MAKES 4 SERVINGS

2 large eggs
2 inches fresh turmeric root, peeled and roughly chopped; or 1 tablespoon ground turmeric
One 15-ounce tub whole milk ricotta cheese, drained in cheesecloth for 15 minutes
2/3 cup freshly grated Parmigiano-Reggiano cheese
2 tablespoons butter, melted and cooled slightly, plus 1½ tablespoons for the sauté pan
¼ teaspoon freshly grated nutmeg
1½ cups "00" pasta flour, or more as needed
¼ cup poppy seeds (optional)
Kosher salt
1 tablespoon olive oil

1. Combine the eggs and turmeric in a blender and blend on low speed, slowly increasing speed until a smooth puree forms.

2. In a medium bowl, mix the puree, ricotta, Parmigiano, melted butter, and nutmeg with a rubber spatula until uniform. Slowly fold in the flour and poppy seeds (if using), just until the mixture pulls away from the sides of the bowl. Do not overmix or add too much flour or your gnudi will be tough. Sprinkle

flour over the mixture until the outsides are all coated and not sticking to the bowl.

3. Line a sheet pan with parchment paper and flour the parchment generously. Flour your hands and gently tear off a 1-inch chunk of dough (or you can use a small scoop to portion out your chunks more evenly). Roll the dough between your floured palms just until a ball forms; it should be nearly the size of a Ping-Pong ball. Do not over-roll or

you'll wind up with tough gnudi. Place the dough ball on the sheet pan and repeat to roll the rest of the dough. Strive for uniformity in size. If some are bigger or smaller, you will wind up with some that are mushy and overcooked and some that are liquidy inside.

4. Cover the sheet pan and refrigerate immediately for at least 30 minutes so they have a chance to firm up. This pasta does not store well, so I recommend cooking within 3 hours.

5. Bring a generous amount of salted water to a boil in a large pot over high heat and, in a large sauté pan over medium heat, heat the oil and the remaining 1½ tablespoons butter.

6. Boil half of the gnudi until they float, 3 to 5 minutes. Gently stir the gnudi occasionally with a wooden spoon to keep them from sticking to the bottom of the pot. Test the gnudi for doneness by removing one with a slotted spoon and cutting it in half. If it looks (and tastes) cooked through, they are done. Repeat with the remaining gnudi.

7. Gently remove the gnudi with a large slotted spoon or spider and brown them in the sauté pan until slightly firm on all sides, about 4 minutes. You may have to do this in batches if your sauté pan is not large enough. Toss with sauce or cheese and serve immediately.

5

FROM TOP TO BOTTOM:
Sage Browned Butter (page 202), Walnut and Poppy Seed
Browned Butter (page 205), Paprika Browned Butter (page 204),
Thyme Browned Butter (page 203)

SAUCES

Have you ever been overwhelmed by a menu? Nothing is worse than stepping into a restaurant for a relaxing night out and being handed a veritable tome, with page after page of choices, each so incongruous from the last that you wonder how one establishment could possibly make so many things. The proof, inevitably, is in the pudding, when you receive your chosen poison only to discover that it's lackluster at best, and now that you're noticing, the Thai lettuce wraps look suspiciously like the Vietnamese summer rolls, and they taste the same too.

I developed the sauce recipes in this chapter with just the opposite of that in mind. I aimed for clean and concise, like a chalkboard menu in a restaurant with entrées based on what's fresh, ripe, and seasonal.

Different regions in Italy specialize in different pasta shapes, and often you'll see a certain noodle paired with a specific sauce because that's how it's been done for centuries, and also because the sauce was designed to hug that particular kind of noodle. Examples include *Trofie al Pesto*, a Ligurian staple, or *Tagliatelle alla Bolognese*, a classic from Emilia-Romagna.

Italians are not thoughtlessly strict about what pasta goes with what sauce. After all, culturally they've been making these pairings for a long time, most emphatically for the past century and a half. What we think of as cooking technique is really the marriage of science and art, and while the art can change to accommodate modern preferences, the science remains. I'm mindful of that when suggesting sauce pairings, of course with a nod to contemporary taste.

Italians think of sauce as clothing for pasta; the ideal amount of sauce should be no more or no less than just the right amount, and if you wonder what that means, think about how you dress yourself each day. This is also a seasonal concept; in the winter you wear heavier clothes, just as in pasta you eat heavier sauces, such as a rich ragù that isn't appropriate in the height of summer.

A common mistake outside of Italy is to lay a bed of noodles down and then ladle sauce on top. Back to the clothing analogy—you wouldn't just toss a dress on top of your head and leave the house; you'd put it on and make sure all its creases hug all your creases in just the right way before you take it for a public spin. Similarly, pasta needs to be tossed in sauce and then placed on the plate—that way you know you have the ratio of noodles to sauce just right.

I did have to balance that concept with the sheer beauty of the noodles in this book. While some of us might make these pastas for nutrition and fun, most of us also want the spoils of our labor to be noticed by our dinner guests, not buried under mounds of chunky sauce. I tried to keep the sauces on the translucent side when possible, so even if a noodle is thoroughly coated, it will still peek out prettily from the plate. Ultimately you should use your best judgment when mixing your noodles with sauce, but keep this in mind as a guide for your steady saucing hand.

Since so much of this book is about the pasta itself, I wanted the sauces to sing, but not as obnoxiously as an off-key soprano in an extended aria. Sauce and pasta should work together like members of the Village People, in sync and on key, with jazz hands inserted when the joy is just too much to contain.

I want to share some general ideas about how I approach sauces in the hope that they'll offer you some clarity as you cook these recipes.

UNPEELED VEGETABLES

Unless I've noted otherwise in a specific recipe, I do not personally peel vegetables and fruits such as apples, potatoes, celery, or carrots. Our family grows some of our own produce, and what we don't grow, we get from farmer friends, the farmers' market, or natural foods stores. There's plenty of controversy surrounding the presence of pesticides in produce, and I'm not going to enter the fray, as I'm no scientist. I will say that I trust my sources and I believe there's flavor and nutrition in peels. That said, if I were using a conventionally grown apple from the grocery store, I would probably peel it. I'm sharing this to give you the gentle nudge to use your best judgment. If you think something needs to be peeled, by all means, peel it.

BUTTER

I use European-style cultured butter in almost all sauce recipes that call for butter. I prefer butter that has a high fat content, the tang of culturing, and as a bonus, the earthy notes present when it is grass-fed. The salt content matters less to me because I can always adjust that at the end of cooking. All of these recipes were tested using European-style cultured butter; Kerrygold makes a readily available one, but feel free to use your own preferred butter.

QUANTO BASTA

If you've spent much time perusing Italian cookbooks or recipe blogs, you've undoubtedly come across the phrase *quanto basta* (often written "Q.B."), essentially meaning as much as needed, or just enough. In my own kitchen, I cook *quanto basta*, meaning I add a pinch of this, just enough of that, let it all come together, and then taste it toward the end of cooking to make sure the flavors fuse. If they don't, I'll add a little more salt, a touch of pepper, some acid in the form of balsamic vinegar or reduced wine, a bit more sweetness via fresh small tomatoes or dried stone fruits, and so on.

The key here is that I'm adding and correcting to get the dish to taste the way *I* want it to taste, not the way it reads in a recipe. The page is flat; your palate is as deep, nuanced, and personalized as your G-spot. The habanero that has you hot and bothered is not the fennel that frenzies me.

Since *quanto basta* is such a nebulous concept, for the most part I put concise measurements in this book that will take readers 95 percent of the way there. I would encourage you to crest your own wave over that last 5 percent; explore your taste preferences as you would a new lover, and experiment. By playing around enough, you'll eventually learn to cook by feel, not by rote, and your most magical kitchen creations will come as a result.

The only instance in which I've employed the use of *quanto basta* is when I've suggested a sprinkling of Parmigiano-Reggiano or Pecorino Romano atop a plated dish. If you see "freshly grated Parmigiano-Reggiano, Q.B." at the end of an ingredients list, it just means to use as much as you like, preferably freshly grated at the table.

SUBSTITUTIONS

If I call for a particular cheese, cured meat, or type of tomato, I do so for a reason, but that's no reason for you to not make the recipe just because you can't find it or maybe don't like it. Tweak these sauce recipes with what you can find and what you like.

That being said, if I specify ground pork and you slide in eggplant, your sauce is going to have some structural flaws. Try to stay within a family when substituting—for example, using prosciutto instead of speck, or leeks instead of onions.

If you're ever going to truly love spending time in the kitchen, it needs to be a relatively stress-free, chill experience, and a sweaty morning spent in white-knuckled traffic hunting from fromagerie to market stall for ingredients is the total opposite of Zen. Come prepared, but be flexible, or, in the immortal words of Bobby McFerrin, don't worry, be happy.

TIMING

I already touched on timing in the "Everything You Need to Know About Cooking Your Stunning Noodles" section on page 64, and you might want to give it a once-over, especially regarding how to time sauce making with pasta cooking. I'll

add a few sauce-specific hints for timing here.

Please make sure you have everything you need chopped, sliced, diced, and ready to go on the counter before you start a sauce recipe. Many of the sauces come together quickly, and you'll be a lot less frazzled if you don't have to pause what you're doing to unearth an ingredient from the pantry.

Read, and even reread, the entire recipe before you start a sauce. Little details like when to put something in the pot can trip you up, and adding things in the order they're meant to be added will make a difference in the end.

The salient takeaway on timing is this: The more prepared you are at the beginning, the more effortless the "during" slog will feel—and the more marvelous the final sauce will be.

SPICE GRINDER

If you don't already own one, invest in a small, inexpensive spice grinder, sometimes marketed as a coffee grinder. There's no need to spend more than $20 on it, and that is one Andrew Jackson that will pay itself back in spades. I use it many times per day. It's helpful to grind spices together before rubbing them on cuts of meat, even if they're already powdered, because it ensures an evenly mixed rub. Preground pepper has hardly any flavor, whereas freshly ground peppercorns put a little boogie in the butts of even the plainest of Janes. I even pulverize things like garlic, parsley, and thyme if I'm really pressed for time and don't want to dirty a cutting board.

INDUCTION HEAT

I live with my family of three humans, two dogs, thirteen ducks, and *mumble mumble* chickens (okay, more than thirty, less than forty, leave me alone, they're my friends!) on five acres in the woods east of Seattle, Washington. We lucked into our property and subsequently completed construction on a copper-clad home with a modern design through a series of DIY misadventures that deserve a book unto themselves. As you can probably imagine, my favorite part was designing and building the kitchen.

I wanted it to be a functional, open space I could use to cook for large dinner parties, and occasionally from which to teach pasta-making workshops. Because of the latter, I got it into my head that I needed two of everything—two pasta stations, two sinks, and two stoves. That way I could demonstrate something, and there would be plenty of space for students to work as well. Between wielding a nail gun and sawing tile, my husband and I made the rounds of the

home show circuit—Dwell on Design was our favorite—and researched the latest and greatest in kitchen appliances. I saw so many stoves, cooktops, dishwashers, espresso machines, fridges, and wall ovens that I started dreaming in owner's-manualese.

One of my biggest mental debates was whether to get a gas or induction cooktop. I had always cooked on gas in the past, but the ease of use, cleanliness, and efficiency of induction intrigued me. In the end, all that trade show traipsing paid off when we realized we could get deep discounts on floor models if we made offers at the end of the shows. While two of everything is twice as nice, it's also twice the price, so it softened the blow considerably when we outfitted our entire kitchen at 50 percent off.

I ultimately couldn't decide on gas or induction, so I got both—one gas four-burner plus griddle and a newfangled induction contraption. It doesn't have burners or even zones—you just place the pot on the cooktop and the unit senses where the pot is through magnetic technology and heats only that area. It detects the size and shape of the pot, so you get even heat whether your pot is oval, rectangular, tiny, round, or enormous.

I've been cooking over both kinds of heat for four years, and I use the induction cooktop 90 percent of the time. I can't say it's better for everyone, but as someone who cooks a lot of pasta and sauce and makes stock from scratch, it's best for me. It boils water like a dream and keeps sauces at the lowest simmer imaginable for exactly as long as I want them to cook. This means that I can start a sauce and stock, and if I need to walk away, I can set a specific cook time and temperature for each pot separately. When the time has elapsed, the magnetic heating coils under whichever pot is finished will turn off, and the other one will simmer away until its timer runs out as well.

This is a roundabout way of saying that all the sauces that follow were developed using an induction cooktop. I did test the recipes on gas, and my independent recipe testers made them on gas. I am confident they will work with whatever cooktop you choose, even over the open flame of a campfire.

That being said, if you're cooking on gas, be mindful of the liquid level of the sauce and add a little more water or stock if it looks like it's evaporating quickly. A flame tamer will help a gas burner to come down to a true simmer. If you have any questions about induction, reach out to me, as I've become somewhat of an accidental evangelist.

USING PASTA WATER IN BROWNED BUTTER SAUCES

All the recipes using browned butter require you to form an emulsion by whisking starchy pasta water with butter until you achieve a uniform sauce. If you're not boiling batch after batch of pasta, your water may not be starchy enough. Please add 1 tablespoon semolina flour per quart of water to achieve the right starch content in your pasta water. Make this addition when you add the pasta to the water. If you do it sooner, your water will boil over if you're not attentive.

SAGE BROWNED BUTTER

This sauce sings, despite its simplicity. I love to experience flavor purity in excellent, if easy, food. It's all about the supporting cast—butter, nutmeg, and balsamic—working harmoniously to let the sage take center stage in the least diva-driven way. Its versatility means that this sauce is equally at home with whisper-thin tajarin or drizzled over egg yolk ravioloni. MAKES 4 SERVINGS | PREPARATION TIME: 15 MINUTES

6 tablespoons butter
14 fresh sage leaves, chopped into chiffonade
¼ teaspoon freshly grated nutmeg
4 teaspoons balsamic vinegar
1 cup hot, starchy pasta water (important—see the note on using pasta water in browned butter sauces on page 201)
½ cup freshly grated Parmigiano-Reggiano cheese, plus more Q.B. for topping plates of pasta

1. Melt the butter over medium heat in a large sauté pan. Continue cooking the butter until it turns a light golden brown, keeping a vigilant eye on it. Add the sage and continue cooking until the butter turns medium golden brown and smells nutty, about 2 minutes more. Remove the pan from the heat for 1 minute.

2. Add the nutmeg and vinegar and return the pan to medium-high heat, stirring to combine. Immediately add the pasta water and Parmigiano and whisk until the cheese disappears and the sauce starts to thicken, about 1 to 2 minutes.

3. Toss with pasta and serve immediately, topping each plate with additional cheese, if desired.

THYME BROWNED BUTTER

Anyone who has ever worked prep in a professional kitchen knows the pain of "doin' thyme," or picking thousands upon thousands of tiny thyme leaves off their pesky stems. When you're doing so for this recipe, take a moment to offer solidarity to professional cooks everywhere who are doin' their own thyme and be thankful you have to pick only enough for four servings.

This recipe calls for verjus, which is a sort of vinegar made from unripened grapes that a winemaker doesn't want to cut off the vine and leave to rot. It's a product that appeals to my deep love of the *cucina povera* concept, which is to waste not, and focus on coaxing elegant flavors from ingredients that might have otherwise gone ignored.

MAKES 4 SERVINGS | PREPARATION TIME: 15 MINUTES

½ cup verjus (substitute apple cider vinegar if you cannot find verjus)
6 tablespoons butter
1 heaping tablespoon fresh thyme leaves
1 garlic clove, minced
1 cup hot, starchy pasta water (important—see the note on using pasta water in browned butter sauces on page 201)
½ cup freshly grated Parmigiano-Reggiano cheese, plus more Q.B. for topping plates of pasta

1. In a small saucepan, cook the verjus over medium heat until reduced to ¼ cup, about 3 minutes.

2. Meanwhile, melt the butter in a large sauté pan over medium heat. Continue cooking until the butter turns a light golden brown, keeping a vigilant eye on it. Reduce the heat to medium-low and add the thyme and garlic. Continue cooking until the butter turns medium golden brown and smells nutty, about 2 minutes

more. Remove the pan from the heat for 1 minute. Add the verjus and return the pan to medium heat, stirring to combine. Add the pasta water and Parmigiano and whisk until the cheese disappears and the sauce starts to thicken, about 1 to 2 minutes.

3. Toss with pasta and serve immediately, topping each plate with additional cheese, if desired.

PAPRIKA BROWNED BUTTER

This browned butter boasts the benefit of an unlikely ally to the paprika: Pecorino Romano cheese. Pecorino is made from sheep's milk, which has 60 percent more protein and a higher fat content than cow's milk, resulting in a rich, piquant cheese. Pecorino plays against the sweet, spicy notes of the paprika to make a culinary power couple. All they need is a cloying couple's name—how about Pecorika?

A note on paprika: Buy the freshest paprika you can find, and if it's been sitting in your spice cabinet for more than a few months, toss it. Over time, paprika loses that special oomph and eventually tastes more like ash than sass. It would be a real shame to use something substandard to make such a simple sauce that relies on great ingredients. MAKES 4 SERVINGS | PREPARATION TIME: 15 MINUTES

> 6 tablespoons butter
> 1 tablespoon sweet Hungarian paprika
> 1 cup hot, starchy pasta water (important—see the note on using pasta water in browned butter sauces on page 201)
> 1 cup freshly grated Pecorino Romano cheese, plus more Q.B. for topping plates of pasta
> 1 teaspoon lemon zest grated on a Microplane
> 1 tablespoon freshly squeezed lemon juice

1. Melt the butter over medium heat in a large sauté pan. Continue cooking until the butter turns a light golden brown, keeping a vigilant eye on it. Stir in the paprika and continue cooking for 2 minutes, or until the butter smells sweet and nutty. Add the pasta water, pecorino, and lemon zest and juice and whisk until the cheese disappears and the sauce starts to thicken, about 1 to 2 minutes.

2. Toss with pasta and serve immediately, topping each plate with additional cheese, if desired.

WALNUT AND POPPY SEED BROWNED BUTTER

This browned butter accomplishes a lot of things. It's firmly on the savory side, yet it incorporates some sweeter flavors that lend balance to the sauce. The nuts add structure, and the garam masala satisfies nostalgic yearnings you didn't even know you had. After you make it once, you'll be able to close your eyes and experience this sauce every time you dream of it. For me, that is often.

MAKES 4 SERVINGS | PREPARATION TIME: 15 MINUTES

6 tablespoons butter
½ cup roughly chopped walnuts
2 tablespoons poppy seeds
¼ teaspoon garam masala
1 teaspoon honey
1 teaspoon apple cider vinegar
1 cup hot, starchy pasta water (important—see the note on using pasta water in browned butter sauces on page 201)

1. Melt the butter over medium heat in a large sauté pan. Continue cooking until it turns a light golden brown, keeping a vigilant eye on it. Stir in the walnuts and cook for 1 minute. Add the poppy seeds and garam masala and cook for 1 minute. Stir the honey and vinegar into the nuts and seeds. Increase the heat to medium-high and whisk the pasta water into the butter for about 2 minutes, or until the sauce begins to thicken.

2. Toss with pasta and serve immediately.

BRODO DI PARMIGIANO

This recipe is *cucina povera* in a stockpot—after all, it makes deeply flavorful *brodo* or broth out of something that most people would throw away, the hard rinds of Parmigiano-Reggiano cheese. While it's true that it takes 5½ hours to make, it will be an entirely pleasant way to pass the time, since the perfume enveloping your kitchen is of the most intoxicating sort.

If ever a smell could be mellifluous, this is it. Prepare to be hungry and wish to dip anything and everything in that shimmering pot as the flavors collide into one another like young lovers reunited after months apart.

Any pasta in the book is an acceptable match for this broth, because while it's on the thin side as far as sauces go, it's no delicate wallflower. The gut shot of umami it packs can stand up to the heartiest of noodles, or the most filamentary.

MAKES 2 QUARTS BRODO | PREPARATION TIME: 5½ HOURS (MOSTLY INACTIVE)

1 pound Parmigiano-Reggiano cheese rinds*
1 small, hard Italian sausage (5 to 7 ounces) such as Creminelli's
    Sopressata, Casalingo, Barolo, or Wild Boar, sliced into 1-inch pieces
    (vegetarians: omit)
2 yellow onions, peeled and coarsely chopped
2 russet potatoes, coarsely chopped
2 carrots, coarsely chopped
1 garlic head, halved crosswise
13 bay leaves
11 fresh thyme sprigs
1 tablespoon whole black peppercorns
1 tablespoon kosher salt
1 teaspoon juniper berries
1 bunch fresh parsley

Save your parm rinds in the refrigerator. When you have a pound, make this rich nectar, or if your need is urgent, substitute hunks of actual Parmigiano-Reggiano.

1. Add everything but the parsley to a large stockpot with 3 quarts water. Bring to a boil, then reduce the heat to a simmer so low you see only a bubble every 10 seconds or so. Maintain this simmer for 4 hours, stirring occasionally.

2. Add the parsley and simmer for 1 more hour. Strain all of the solids out of the stock with a sieve over a bowl and use the broth immediately, or store in the refrigerator for up to 5 days, or the freezer for up to 1 month

NOTE: To make a soup-like pasta dish, boil the pasta directly in the broth along with greens such as kale, bok choy, or broccoli.

NOTE: To make a thicker sauce to coat noodles, simmer to reduce the brodo by half, then toss it with pasta just before serving.

FAST, FRESH TOMATO SAUCE WITH RICOTTA SALATA

Don't let the elegant purity of this sauce deceive you. It's rich, balanced, and umami-laden despite coming together in less than half an hour. I tell people I love tomatoes too much to eat them outside of August; after all, not much beats a sun-ripened tomato. A December hothouse facsimile just doesn't compare. Nevertheless, I made it my mission to develop a sauce that is just as magical in the dead of winter as it is during harvest, and the use of teeny tiny flavor bomb tomatoes here was key.

Ricotta salata is a cheese worth seeking. It's salted and pressed sheep's milk ricotta originating in southern Italy. It has a tangy, bright flavor that rounds out the sweetness of the sauce. MAKES 4 SERVINGS | PREPARATION TIME: 25 MINUTES

4 ounces pancetta, chopped
3 garlic cloves, minced
1 anchovy fillet, minced
⅓ cup balsamic vinegar
1 pound small tomatoes, sometimes labeled sugar plum or grape
    (roughly 3 cups)
½ cup jarred julienned sun-dried tomatoes, drained
1½ cups chicken stock
1 teaspoon kosher salt
¼ teaspoon freshly ground black pepper
1 cup loosely packed fresh basil leaves
8 ounces ricotta salata cheese, grated on the large holes of a box grater

1. In a large sauté pan over medium heat, fry the pancetta for 5 minutes, or until most of the fat has rendered. Add the garlic and anchovy and sauté for 30 seconds, until the garlic is fragrant, stirring constantly. Add the vinegar and cook for 2 minutes, until slightly syrupy, stirring occasionally. Increase the heat to high and add the fresh and sun-dried tomatoes, stock, and salt. Cover and cook for 5 minutes without opening the lid to peek (the sauce will sputter angrily at you if you do—ask me how I know). Reduce the heat to medium-low and cook for 1 minute. Remove the lid and stir; the sauce will be bright, with a slightly jammy texture. Add the pepper.

2. Remove from the heat and stir in the basil and ricotta salata. Toss with pasta and serve immediately.

Fast, Fresh Tomato Sauce with Ricotta Salata (page 209) pictured with Two-Toned Fettucine (page 96)

BACON-PEANUT-TOMATO SAUCE

I have always been a peanut-aholic. In fact, rare, expensive, chalky, substandard peanut butter was one of the harder things to get used to when I lived in Italy. Only in recent years, however, have I discovered just how well peanuts pair with tomatoes. Throw bacon in and this becomes an *if this is wrong I don't wanna be right* kind of sauce.

If you're looking for a pasta–sauce matchup that is like the hottest Tinder hookup ever, pair this with Beet Gnocchi (page 174).

MAKES 4 SERVINGS | PREPARATION TIME: 15 MINUTES

12 ounces bacon, cut into ¼-inch pieces
1 leek, trimmed and rinsed carefully, white part sliced into ⅛-inch
  rings
1 pound grape tomatoes
2/3 cup roasted, salted peanuts, finely chopped
1 tablespoon fresh thyme leaves
½ teaspoon kosher salt
¼ teaspoon freshly ground black pepper
½ cup dry or amontillado sherry
¾ cup hot, starchy pasta water
2 loosely packed cups pea sprouts or other tender greens

1. Fry the bacon in a large saucepan over medium-high heat until the edges begin to crisp, about 5 minutes. Pour off all but 2 tablespoons of the bacon fat. (If you're serving this with beet gnocchi, use the bacon fat in the baking dish when you crisp up the gnocchi.)

2. Stir in the leek and sauté for 2 minutes. Add the tomatoes, peanuts, thyme, salt, and pepper and stir to combine. Cook for 2 minutes, then add the sherry and scrape any bits off the bottom of the pan. When the sherry has nearly evaporated, about 2 minutes, add the pasta water and bring to a blustering boil for 1 minute.

3. Remove from the heat. Carefully add pasta and gently toss. Serve immediately, topping each portion with a handful of pea sprouts.

ROASTED TOMATOES WITH BASIL OIL AND BURRATA

This sauce honors the elements of a caprese salad—tomato, mozzarella, and basil. It's a celebrated flavor combo for a reason, and that reason is to make your mouth sing with the flavors of Italy on a warm spring evening. I'll never forget the first time I had a truly remarkable caprese. I was nineteen, sitting in an outdoor restaurant in a boisterous piazzetta on the balmy Italian island of Capri. While I thought I had tasted caprese before, the first bite showed me what I was missing with supermarket tomatoes, lackluster basil, and rubbery mozzarella.

So many culinary combinations in Italy come from few ingredients, and yet their flavor is mighty. That is because the building blocks are of the very highest quality. I'd love it if you would try to select the freshest basil and burrata and the ripest tomatoes you can find to make this sauce. Trust me, your dinner guests will love it too.

This sauce highlights really pretty pasta, because even though there's a lot going on, it's not terribly visually distracting from the noodles themselves. Something like Striped Paccheri Rigati (page 144) would work delightfully.

It also wins points for flexibility. Dress it up by dolloping a spoonful of caviar on each portion, or make it humble by substituting mozzarella balls for the burrata. If you can't find mini-roma tomatoes, feel free to use another medium-small, sweet tomato variety, preferably home- or trusted farmer-grown.

Blanching any greens with a bit of baking soda in the water helps them to maintain their vibrant color.   MAKES 4 SERVINGS | PREPARATION TIME: 45 MINUTES

BASIL OIL
1 teaspoon kosher salt
½ teaspoon baking soda
4 ounces fresh basil, both leaves and stems (reserve a few leaves
    for garnish)
⅔ cup extra-virgin olive oil

WHOLE ROASTED TOMATOES
12 ounces mini Roma tomatoes (or small vine tomatoes or
    Campari tomatoes)
3 tablespoons olive oil
10 thyme sprigs
1 tablespoon kosher salt

One 8-ounce tub burrata cheese (2 balls)
½ cup hot, starchy pasta water
Freshly grated Parmigiano-Reggiano cheese, Q.B.

1. To make the basil oil, in a medium saucepan over high heat, bring 4 cups water to a boil with the salt and baking soda. Add the basil and blanch for 10 seconds, then drain immediately. Press as much water out as you can, then blend the basil and oil in a blender until smooth. Pour the basil oil through a fine-mesh strainer into a lidded glass jar. It will take some time for the oil to pass through the mesh, so continue with the rest of the recipe while you wait. (You can make the basil oil up to 1 week ahead, although in my fridge it never lasts more than a day, what with midnight toast dips and such.)

2. To make the whole roasted tomatoes, preheat the oven to 450°F. Put the tomatoes in a large aluminum foil packet along with the oil, thyme, and salt and pinch it tightly closed at the top. Place the packet on a sheet pan to keep the oil from dripping onto the oven floor. Roast for 30 minutes, or until the tomatoes are blistered and soft but not falling apart.

3. To assemble, 1 minute before serving, drain the liquid from the burrata container and pour the hot pasta water over the burrata balls to warm them slightly. Don't immerse them in hot water for more than 1 minute or the burrata will become tough.

4. Toss the whole roasted tomatoes with the pasta, then divide the pasta among four plates, top each portion with ½ ball of burrata, and drizzle on some basil oil. Garnish with the reserved basil leaves and Parmigiano.

BURRATA-SPECK-PEA SAUCE

Nancy Silverton, of Mozza fame, is a culinary idol of mine, and she makes an appetizer with burrata, speck, and peas in *The Mozza Cookbook*. This sauce is a pasta homage to her dish, to spring, and to the old-world Italian combination of peas, Parmigiano-Reggiano, and prosciutto. The big flavors and bold ingredients will overpower a wispy, lithe noodle, so think textured and craggy, such as farfalle or fusilli, when deciding on a pasta pairing for this one.

Labneh is just yogurt that has been drained to remove the whey, resulting in a thick and tangy cream. If you can't find it, substitute drained whole milk yogurt.

MAKES 4 SERVINGS | PREPARATION TIME: 20 MINUTES

2 teaspoons olive oil
1 small shallot, julienned
3 ounces speck (about 10 thin pieces), each piece sliced into
   ¼-inch strips (can substitute prosciutto)
2/3 cup freshly shelled English peas
½ cup labneh
1 tablespoon freshly squeezed lemon juice
½ teaspoon kosher salt
¼ teaspoon freshly ground black pepper
2 tablespoons finely chopped fresh mint
1½ cups hot, starchy pasta water
30 sugar snap peas, stringy ends removed, sliced on the bias into
   ¼-inch pieces
One 8-ounce tub burrata cheese (2 balls), drained
½ cup pea sprouts or tender vines of young peas (optional)
Freshly grated Parmigiano-Reggiano cheese, Q.B. (optional)

1. Heat the oil in a large sauté pan over medium heat. Fry the shallot for 2 minutes, then add the speck and fry for 2 minutes more. Increase the heat to medium-high, add the peas, labneh, lemon juice, salt, pepper, mint, and 1 cup of the pasta water. Stir and bring to a boil. Reduce the heat to a low simmer and toss immediately with pasta and half of the sugar snap peas.

Pictured with Polka-Dot
Farfalle (page 118)

2. One minute before serving, pour the remaining ½ cup hot pasta water over the burrata balls. Plate the pasta and top with the remaining sugar snap peas. Gently remove the burrata from the hot water and tear each ball in half using your hands. Place half a burrata on top of each serving of pasta along with the pea sprouts (if using). Top with the Parmigiano, if desired.

PECORINO-PEPPER SAUCE WITH BROCCOLINI

Readers familiar with *cacio e pepe*, a pillar of Roman *primi piatti*, will note the nod to it here. Since there is no improving perfect, rather than offering my interpretation, I rolled those flavors into something different. The result is punchy pecorino twirled with pepper, garlic, and bits of broccolini that mingle best with strands of thin pasta, such as tajarin. If ever there was luxury in simplicity, it would be at the bottom of a bowl of this.

MAKES 4 SERVINGS | PREPARATION TIME: 20 MINUTES

8 ounces Pecorino Romano cheese
2 tablespoons butter
1 tablespoon olive oil
1 bunch broccolini (about 8 ounces), cut into ½-inch pieces
1⅓ cups hot, starchy pasta water
1 tablespoon freshly ground black pepper
2 garlic cloves, minced

1. Chop the pecorino into 1-inch pieces (if you have a full-size, high-speed blender) or grate it (if you have a regular blender). Place the cheese in the blender.

2. Heat the butter and oil in a sauté pan over medium-high heat. Add the broccolini and cook for 3 minutes, until it just begins to wilt, stirring occasionally.

3. Meanwhile, puree the cheese and the pasta water in the blender until homogeneous. Be sure the lid is on tight, as pureeing hot liquids can be dangerous.

4. Add the pepper and garlic to the broccolini and cook for 1 to 2 minutes, until the aroma of pepper and garlic fills the air.

5. Pour the pecorino–pasta water puree into the broccolini and stir to combine, then immediately toss the mixture well with pasta, making sure every noodle is coated in sauce. Serve immediately.

Pecorino-Pepper Sauce with Broccolini
(page 219) pictured with Hand-Cut
Tajarin (page 88)

APPLE BACON SAUCE

I'm not sure it's possible to make a more nontraditional pasta sauce in Italian terms out of more traditionally combined ingredients than bacon, apples, and sage. This sauce might have an Italian nonna rolling over in her *tomba*, but a British one would be lapping this up faster than you can say "Who's your nan?" I heartily recommend it with any pasta that is stuffed with butternut squash filling, as the squash-bacon-apple combo adds a whole new dimension. MAKES 4 SERVINGS | PREPARATION TIME: 20 MINUTES

12 ounces bacon, cut into ¼-inch pieces
1 small red onion, julienned
7 fresh sage leaves, chiffonaded
1 not-too-sweet sweet apple, such as Gala, Braeburn, or Pink Lady, cut
    into ¼-inch dice
½ teaspoon prepared yellow mustard
1½ cups chicken stock or hot, starchy pasta water
¼ teaspoon ground white pepper
¼ teaspoon freshly grated nutmeg
1 teaspoon flaky salt, such as Murray River or Maldon
1 cup finely grated sharp Cheddar cheese

1. In a medium saucepan over medium heat, fry the bacon for 2 minutes, until slightly rendered. Add the onion and sauté for 2 minutes, until softened, stirring once or twice. Add the sage and fry for 1 minute. Add the apple and mustard and sauté for 2 minutes, stirring frequently.

2. Increase the heat to medium-high and deglaze the pan with the stock, scraping any browned bits off the bottom of the pan. Bring to a simmer and reduce the heat to medium-low. Stir in the white pepper, nutmeg, and salt and simmer for 2 minutes, then reduce the heat to low.

3. The sauce can be served immediately but will hold for 15 minutes on the lowest setting on your stove. Just before serving, add the Cheddar and stir to combine. Toss with pasta and serve immediately.

Pictured with Lattice-Patterned Caramelle (page 150)

COLD NOODLE DIPPING SAUCE

More often than not, we think of pasta as a dish best served warm, but that need not be the case. In the heat of summer, on a picnic, or when you want something make-ahead to pull and eat straight from the fridge, cold noodles are the answer. If you skim the ingredients, you'll note the Japanese influence on this sauce, but cold noodles are historically pervasive throughout Italy as well. There they are usually served as part of an *insalata,* but never with mayonnaise, as is common in the United States.

This recipe includes specific cooking instructions for the pasta, because when noodles are destined for a cold preparation, they must be treated differently. The two chief differences are the inclusion of additional salt in the boiling water and the immediate cold shocking of the noodles in a water bath. The extra salt is there because some gets washed off during shocking, and the water bath stops the pasta from cooking further, since there are few worse textures than a soggy cold noodle.

The noodles and sauce are excellent as is, but if you want to gussy them up, thinly slice and serve with an assortment of raw, in-season vegetables. Complementary vegetable pairings include sugar snap peas, beets, radishes, carrots, cabbage, ginger, cilantro, and cucumbers. MAKES 4 SERVINGS | PREPARATION TIME: 40 MINUTES

DIPPING SAUCE
1 cup chicken stock
¼ teaspoon fish sauce
1 tablespoon mirin
¼ cup tamari
1 tablespoon rice vinegar
1 teaspoon whole black peppercorns
2 inches fresh ginger root, peeled and sliced into ¼-inch rounds
2 inches fresh turmeric root, peeled and sliced into ¼-inch rounds
1 tablespoon sesame oil, spicy if you prefer

PASTA
6 tablespoons kosher salt
1 batch fresh pasta of your choice (I would recommend noodles fettuccine-thickness or thinner; chitarra noodles are particularly nice)
2 tablespoons olive oil
2 tablespoons sesame seeds (optional)

1. To make the dipping sauce, in a small saucepan over medium heat, combine all the ingredients *except the sesame oil* and bring the mixture to a simmer. Immediately turn the heat to the lowest possible setting; use a flame tamer if you're cooking on a powerful gas range, as you're looking for a true simmer here. Cover and cook for 30 minutes. Remove from the heat and strain with a sieve into a serving bowl; discard the solids. Add the sesame oil and serve immediately or store, covered, in the refrigerator, for up to 1 week.

2. To make the pasta, combine 4 quarts water and the salt in a large pot over high heat and prepare a large bowl of ice water. When the water is boiling, add the pasta and cook for 1 minute, or until al dente. Drain and shock the noodles in ice water until they are cool and not stuck together. Drain the noodles and toss them thoroughly in the oil, topping with sesame seeds if desired.

3. The noodles can be served alongside the dipping sauce at this point, or kept in the refrigerator for up to 24 hours. They are meant to be dipped in the sauce bite by bite, so plating each portion with a small ramekin of sauce is ideal.

BUTTERNUT SQUASH AND GOAT CHEESE SAUCE WITH PINE NUTS

This is a novice sauce that packs an expert punch of flavor. It will happily hug just about any noodle, but I'm especially fond of it with either or both of the bright, colorful gnudi recipes on pages 187 and 192. The sauce is velvety and robust, but you won't feel weighed down eating it because it's not nearly as heavy as a roux-based cheese sauce.

MAKES 4 GENEROUS SERVINGS | PREPARATION TIME: 30 MINUTES

One 2- to 3-pound butternut squash, peeled and cut into ½-inch cubes
⅔ cup pine nuts
1 tablespoon chopped fresh thyme
1 teaspoon kosher salt
½ teaspoon freshly ground black pepper
½ teaspoon sweet Hungarian paprika
2 tablespoons olive oil
2 cups chicken stock
10½ ounces plain goat cheese
Grated zest and juice of 2 lemons (Meyer preferred)
1 tablespoon chopped fresh mint
Freshly grated Parmigiano-Reggiano cheese, Q.B.

1. Preheat the oven to 450°F. Combine the squash, pine nuts, thyme, salt, pepper, paprika, and oil in a medium-size oven-safe casserole dish. Cover it with aluminum foil and roast for 15 minutes, stirring once halfway through.

2. Bring the stock to a boil in a medium saucepan. Add the squash mixture and simmer over medium heat for 7 minutes, until the squash is soft. Set aside to cool for 5 minutes, then puree the mixture in a blender until smooth.

3. Return the puree to the saucepan over low heat and whisk in the goat cheese and lemon zest and juice. Continue whisking until the sauce is smooth and no chunks of cheese remain, about 3 to 5 minutes. You may add a little water if you would like sauce with a thinner consistency.

4. Remove from the heat and stir in the mint. Serve tossed with pasta and top each serving with Parmigiano.

LEMON CREAM SAUCE

If you want to do me a colossal favor, you will make this sauce and serve it with Mint Pea Gnocchi (page 178). And that was my attempt at reverse-psychology to get you to think you're doing me a favor, when really, it is I who is doing you the favor of elevating your dinner to *hot-air balloon ride at sunset with a bottle of Barolo* level.

If I've just pulled some slender carrots from the garden (or bought some from a nice farmer), I will high-heat roast them in just olive oil, salt, and pepper and serve a couple balanced beautifully atop each portion.

MAKES 4 SERVINGS | PREPARATION TIME: 20 MINUTES

3 garlic cloves, minced
1 tablespoon butter
1 cup chicken stock
1 cup dry white wine, such as Pinot Grigio
1 tablespoon cornstarch
1 cup heavy cream
Grated zest of 2 lemons
Juice of 3 lemons
¼ teaspoon freshly grated nutmeg
1 teaspoon kosher salt
¼ teaspoon ground white pepper
Freshly grated Pecorino Romano cheese, Q.B.

1. In a medium saucepan over medium heat, sauté the garlic in the butter for 1 minute, until fragrant. Add the stock and wine and let it simmer until reduced to about 1 cup, about 10 minutes.

2. Meanwhile, put the cornstarch in a small bowl and pour in the cream a little at a time, whisking to form a uniform slurry. When the stock mixture is reduced, add the cream mixture to the reduction and turn the heat to medium-low. Stir constantly until the sauce thickens to the consistency of gravy, then reduce the heat to the lowest possible setting. Add the lemon zest, lemon juice, nutmeg, salt, and white pepper and warm over low heat, stirring every minute for 5 minutes, to cook out the cornstarch flavor.

3. Remove from the heat, toss with pasta, and serve immediately with pecorino.

Pictured with Espresso Chestnut Gnocchetti (page 190)

PIEMONTESE CHEESE SAUCE

While no cheese sauce can get away with the "skinny" moniker, this one isn't terribly sinful because it's milk-based rather than cream-based. The addition of gooey Piemontese cheese makes it silky, rich, and smooth. I suggest La Tur, a soft-ripened cheese made from a blend of sheep, cow, and goat's milk. If you cannot find it, look for Taleggio, which is from nearby Lombardia and makes a fine substitute. If these suggestions may as well be Greek (Italian) to you, and your local grocer doesn't carry either of these cheeses, look for something with a soft, creamy consistency, such as a triple-crème Brie. MAKES 4 SERVINGS | PREPARATION TIME: 25 MINUTES

1½ tablespoons butter
1½ tablespoons flour
1½ cups whole milk
8 ounces creamy Piemontese cheese, such as La Tur, rind removed
   (see headnote)
¼ teaspoon freshly grated nutmeg
1 teaspoon flaky salt, such as Murray River or Maldon

1. Melt the butter in a medium saucepan over medium heat. Whisk in the flour and stir with a wooden spoon for 3 minutes, to eliminate the raw flour taste from the finished sauce. Add the milk in a slow, steady stream, whisking vigorously to avoid clumping. When the milk mixture begins to simmer, turn the heat to medium-low and cook for 5 minutes, stirring occasionally. Add the cheese all at once, along with the nutmeg and salt. Reduce the heat to low and stir constantly to melt the cheese into the sauce. The sauce is ready when there are no more clumps of cheese, but it can be held over the lowest heat setting on your stove for 15 minutes.

2. Toss with pasta and serve immediately.

ROSMARINO MAIALE MONDAY SAUCE

I called this Monday sauce because it's easy to throw together even on the most taxing of days, and it is guaranteed to brighten a speedy weeknight meal. There is the idea of a *ragù della Domenica*, or Sunday sauce (sometimes called Sunday gravy) in Italy. To make it, a tireless nonna slaves over a slow-bubbling cauldron all day. This bright and straightforward sauce is the opposite—it takes just a few minutes to prepare—but the punch it packs in flavor will rival the best of the long-simmering/suffering ragùs.

MAKES 4 SERVINGS | PREPARATION TIME: 25 MINUTES

1 tablespoon olive oil
1 tablespoon butter
1 pound ground pork
2 teaspoons kosher salt
1 teaspoon smoky paprika
1 teaspoon onion powder
1 bunch lacinato kale, stems removed, coarsely chopped
3 garlic cloves, minced
Leaves from 2 fresh rosemary sprigs, chopped
2 tablespoons balsamic vinegar
½ cup dry white wine
1 cup hot, starchy pasta water
1 teaspoon red pepper flakes (optional)
One 8-ounce tub mozzarella *ciliegine* (small balls), drained

1. Heat the oil and butter in a large sauté pan over medium-high heat. Add the pork, salt, paprika, and onion powder and cook for 4 minutes, until the pork is browned, stirring with a flat-end wooden spoon to break up clumps. Add the kale and cook for 2 minutes, until wilted, stirring to combine. Reduce the heat to medium, add the garlic and rosemary, and cook for 2 minutes, just long enough to unlock the aromatics. Add the vinegar and wine and use the wooden spoon to scrape any browned bits up off the bottom of the pan. Stir in the pasta water and red pepper flakes (if using) and cook for 2 minutes.

2. Toss with pasta and *ciliegine* 1 minute before serving so that the *ciliegine* retain some of their shape but soften and stretch out a little.

Pictured with
Rigatoni (page 140)

MEYER LEMON AMONTILLADO CHICKEN

This is grown-up lemon chicken that will simultaneously intrigue sophisticated palates and satisfy comfort cravings. I admit that Edgar Allan Poe planted the amontillado seed in me with his haunting short story "The Cask of Amontillado" when I was *way* too young to know what amontillado was, but since I'm something of a sherry fairy these days, it's become a major go-to for both cooking and drinking. When making this, you might consider employing the *one for the pot, one for me* modus operandi. Amontillado is dark, rich, and nutty (I wish someone would describe me that way), so if you must perform a sherry switcheroo, look for those qualities.

Meyer lemons are slightly sweeter and lighter than the average lemon, so seek them out, but don't fret if you have to substitute a regular lemon—it won't make a catastrophic difference. MAKES 4 SERVINGS | PREPARATION TIME: 30 MINUTES

1½ pounds boneless skinless chicken thighs
¼ cup flour
4 teaspoons kosher salt
½ teaspoon freshly ground black pepper
2 tablespoons butter
2 tablespoons olive oil
1 medium red onion, cut into ¼-inch-thick slices
½ cup amontillado sherry
½ teaspoon minced fresh marjoram (a little goes a long way)
1 cup chicken stock
Grated zest and juice of 1 Meyer lemon (about 2 tablespoons juice)
One 12-ounce jar quartered artichoke hearts, drained
½ cup julienned sun-dried tomatoes, drained
½ cup pitted Nicoise olives

1. Cut the chicken thighs into 1-inch strips. In a shallow bowl, combine the flour, salt, and pepper. Dredge the chicken strips in the flour mixture.

2. Heat 1 tablespoon of the butter and 1 tablespoon of the oil in a large sauté pan over medium heat. Add the onion

and sauté until tender, about 4 minutes. Remove from the pan and set aside.

3. Heat the remaining 1 tablespoon butter and 1 tablespoon oil in same pan over medium-high heat. Add the chicken strips and brown them on all sides, about 4 minutes total. Add the sherry

Pictured with Rainbow Cavatelli (page 112)

and marjoram and simmer for 1 minute, scraping any browned bits up off the bottom of the pan. The chicken should be cooked through and the sauce a bit thickened.

4. Turn the heat to medium-low and add the sautéed onions and stock. Cook for 4 minutes, or until the sauce thickens slightly.

5. Turn the heat to low and add the lemon zest and juice, artichoke hearts, sun-dried tomatoes, and olives. Heat through, toss with pasta, and serve immediately.

GOLDEN MILK RAGÙ

Saffron-hued and shimmering, this sauce is senseless to resist. Golden milk is a combination of powerhouse ingredients usually served in the form of tea. Here I've added chicken and slowly coaxed it into a rich, soothing ragù. It's like hippie food and a hug from Mom had a lovechild, and it's as at home tossed with pappardelle as it is carefully ladled over a colorful raviolo.

Adding chanterelle mushrooms sautéed in a little butter to the top of this ragù is a welcome seasonal twist, but I haven't explicitly included them in the recipe because of the fleeting availability of chanterelles. If you're fortunate enough to have some, clean them with a dry brush and sauté them just until soft, in plenty of butter and with a smattering of salt.

MAKES 4 SERVINGS | PREPARATION TIME: 1½ HOURS (BUT IT CAN BE SIMMERED LONGER)

BOUQUET GARNI
5 fresh or dried bay leaves
5 fresh thyme sprigs
½ lemongrass stalk, cut into 1-inch pieces
1 tablespoon whole black peppercorns

CHICKEN AND SAUCE
4 ounces pancetta, cubed
1 tablespoon olive oil
1 pound ground chicken (dark meat if available)
2 teaspoons kosher salt
1 leek, white and light green parts only, rinsed well and sliced into ¼-inch rounds
1 carrot, cut into ¼-inch dice
1 inch fresh ginger root, peeled and minced
3 inches fresh turmeric root, peeled and minced
2 garlic cloves, peeled and minced
1 cup dry white wine
1 cup chicken stock
1½ cups whole milk

1. To make the bouquet garni, enclose the bay leaves, thyme, lemongrass, and peppercorns in cheesecloth and tie the bundle securely with kitchen string. Alternatively, place the herbs in a heatproof tied mesh bag, such as a small nut milk bag.

2. To make the chicken and sauce, fry the pancetta in a heavy-bottomed medium saucepan over medium heat for 3 minutes, or until the fat begins to render.

3. Meanwhile, in a separate large skillet, heat the oil over medium-high heat. Salt the chicken and brown it in the skillet for 4 minutes, breaking up any clumps with a wooden spoon.

4. Add the leek and carrot to the pancetta saucepan and cook, stirring occasionally, for 2 minutes. Add the ginger, turmeric, and garlic and stir to combine.

5. Add the wine to the chicken and scrape any browned bits up off the bottom of the pan. Pour the chicken-wine mixture into the saucepan and add the bouquet garni, taking care to immerse it in the liquid. Bring to a simmer over medium-low heat and cook for 10 minutes, stirring occasionally.

6. Add the stock and milk and bring just to a boil, then immediately turn the heat to low. Simmer uncovered for at least 1 hour and up to 3 hours, adding more stock, or pasta water, if you've simmered toward the longer end and the ragù seems too thick.

7. Just before serving, remove the bouquet garni. Use tongs to squeeze as much liquid from the bouquet garni into the pan as possible, then discard the bouquet garni.

8. This sauce is great on day 1, even better on day 2, and will hold through day 3. Toss with pasta and serve immediately.

POLLO AGRODOLCE

This sauce takes root in Sicily, where a dazzling marriage of Italian and North African ingredients makes food sing. It's historically made with 1 whole rabbit, segmented into pieces small enough to fit into the pan. If you can get your hands on a rabbit, I strongly encourage you to substitute it for the chicken; just be slightly more vigilant about removing any bones before pureeing the sauce, as rabbit does tend to have more fragile bones than chicken.

Pollo Agrodolce is a wonderful accompaniment to cacao noodles (see page 46), especially larger forms such as pappardelle, lasagne, or paccheri.

MAKES 4 SERVINGS | PREPARATION TIME: 2 HOURS

BOUQUET GARNI
7 fresh or dried bay leaves
4 fresh thyme sprigs
5 juniper berries
7 whole black peppercorns

CHICKEN AND SAUCE
4 bone-in, skin-on chicken thighs
1 tablespoon kosher salt
1 tablespoon freshly ground black pepper
1/3 cup flour
2 tablespoons olive oil
2 tablespoons butter
1 carrot, coarsely chopped
1 celery stalk, coarsely chopped
1 small onion, coarsely chopped
3 garlic cloves, minced
3 ounces speck, cut into 1/4-inch pieces (can substitute pancetta)
1 tablespoon packed brown sugar
1/3 cup apple cider vinegar
3 cups chicken stock
11 jarred peppadew peppers, cored: 7 trimmed and halved and
    4 trimmed and cut into 1/8-inch slices
1/3 cup pitted Kalamata olives (reserve a few for garnish)
1/4 cup golden raisins
1/4 cup dried currants or cherries

¼ cup walnuts, toasted (see Note)
3 ounces dark chocolate, chopped
¼ cup pine nuts, toasted (see Note) and chopped
Freshly grated Parmigiano-Reggiano cheese, Q.B.

1. To make the bouquet garni, enclose the bay leaves, thyme, juniper berries, and peppercorns in cheesecloth and tie the bundle securely with kitchen string. Alternatively, place the herbs in a heatproof tied mesh bag, such as a small nut milk bag.

2. To make the chicken and sauce, season the chicken with the salt and pepper, then toss in the flour to coat. Heat the oil and butter in a large sauté pan over medium-high heat and cook the chicken until golden on both sides, about 5 minutes total. Transfer to a plate using tongs.

3. Reduce the heat to medium, add the carrot, celery, and onion, and cook for 4 minutes, stirring occasionally. Add the garlic and speck and cook for 1 minute. Add the bouquet garni, brown sugar, vinegar, and stock and stir to combine. Stir in the 7 halved peppers, the olives, raisins, currants, walnuts, and chocolate. Return the chicken thighs to the pan, skin side up. Bring the liquid to a boil and immediately lower the heat to a simmer, using a flame tamer as necessary. Cook, uncovered, for 1 hour, or until the chicken

is very tender. There should be enough liquid in the pan, but you can add a bit of water if needed.

4. Carefully remove the chicken thighs from the pan and set aside on a plate. Remove the bouquet garni. Use tongs to squeeze as much liquid from the bouquet garni into the pan as possible, then discard the bouquet garni.

5. Optional: If you would like a smooth sauce, use an immersion blender to puree the sauce in the pan, or carefully blend the sauce in a standard mixer, taking care to work in batches so you don't get splattered with hot sauce.

6. Remove the bones and skin from the chicken (it should be very easy at this point) and return the meat to the pan, stirring to heat it through. Toss the sauce with pasta and garnish with the reserved olives and 4 sliced peppers, the pine nuts, and Parmigiano.

NOTE: *To toast nuts, put them on a rimmed baking sheet and bake at 375°F, stirring occasionally, until golden brown, 5 to 10 minutes.*

PORK SHOULDER BRAISED IN MILK AND ROSÉ WITH FIGS

Maiale al latte, or pork braised in milk until the meat becomes tender and juicy, is a common dish in Italy, but the flavor is anything but. This recipe kicks it up a notch with the addition of rosé wine and sweet Mission figs. During the long, slow braise, the sauce separates into golden whey and creamy curds, but it comes back together in the end with a few pulses of the immersion blender.

This recipe makes enough sauce to easily dress two batches of noodles, so be sure to double up on pasta dough. It will actually serve ten people comfortably, not eight, because the sauce is so robust.

You can puree the leftover sauce in the food processor for 10 seconds and use it as a filling in agnolotti, caramelle, or culurgiones. Just put it in a zip-top bag and store it in the fridge or freezer, and when you're ready, snip off the corner of the bag and pipe it into the filled pasta of your choosing. The sauce will pipe best if colder than room temperature. MAKES 10 SERVINGS | PREPARATION TIME: 4½ HOURS

BOUQUET GARNI

10 juniper berries
½ nutmeg seed
4 garlic cloves, unpeeled, halved
3 fresh 6-inch sage sprigs
2 fresh 6-inch rosemary sprigs
6 fresh or dried bay leaves

PORK AND SAUCE

One 3-pound pork shoulder, bone-in (it will most likely be tied in kitchen twine, which is fine)
1 tablespoon kosher salt, plus more as needed
1 teaspoon freshly ground black pepper
1 teaspoon sweet Hungarian paprika
6 ounces bacon, coarsely chopped (about 6 thick-cut slices)
2 onions, coarsely chopped
3 carrots, coarsely chopped
1½ tablespoons Dijon mustard
1 tablespoon packed brown sugar
2 cups dry rosé wine (or a dry white, such as Pinot Grigio)
2 cups whole milk

2 cups chicken stock, or more as needed

10 Mission figs (about 1 basket), quartered (dried figs are also acceptable)

Freshly grated Parmigiano-Reggiano cheese, Q.B.

1. Set the rack at the bottom of the oven and preheat the oven to 300°F.

2. To make a bouquet garni, enclose the juniper berries, nutmeg, garlic, sage, rosemary, and bay leaves in cheesecloth and tie the bundle securely with kitchen string. Alternatively, place the herbs in a heatproof tied mesh bag, such as a small nut milk bag.

3. To make the pork and sauce, season the pork shoulder on all sides with the salt, pepper, and paprika.

4. Put the bacon in a large, heavy-bottomed, oven-proof pan such as a Dutch oven that has an oven-proof, tight-fitting lid. Cook it over medium heat for 3 minutes, until the fat has rendered a little. Tuck the bacon to one side of the pan and increase the heat to medium-high. Add the pork shoulder and brown it on all sides, about 12 minutes total. Lower the heat to medium and add the onions, carrots, mustard, and brown sugar. Stirring occasionally, cook until the onions and carrots are just beginning to soften, about 4 minutes. Add the bouquet garni and the wine to the pan and cook for 4 minutes, until the wine has reduced, then add the milk and stock and bring to a boil. Remove from the heat.

5. Cover the pan, place it in the oven, and braise the pork until it is fall-off-the-bone tender, turning occasionally, 3 to 3½ hours.

6. Remove the pan from the oven and let it cool enough to safely squeeze the juice from the bouquet garni into the pan and discard. Remove the pork to a sheet pan and remove the bone and any kitchen twine.

7. Using an immersion blender, puree the sauce in the pan. If you don't have an immersion blender, you can carefully perform this step in a standard blender, taking care to work in batches so you don't get spattered with hot sauce.

8. Return the pork to the sauce, breaking up any large chunks. Add the figs and bring to a simmer over medium heat. Turn the heat to the lowest level and simmer for at least 30 minutes, or until ready to serve. You can add water or additional stock if the sauce becomes too thick.

9. Just before serving, taste to adjust the seasonings and add salt if necessary. Toss with pasta and serve immediately with Parmigiano-Reggiano.

Pork Shoulder Braised in Milk and Rosé with Figs (page 242)
pictured with Multicolored Garganelli (page 132)

SPICED LAMB YOGURT SAUCE

This sauce bows humbly toward the classic Syrian spread called muhammara, which originated in Aleppo but is now beloved throughout the Middle East and beyond. The flavors are complex and worldly enough to intrigue your most discerning food-loving friends, but warm and approachable too, so that even those with classic preferences will still find this comforting. MAKES 4 SERVINGS | PREPARATION TIME: 45 MINUTES

1 teaspoon ground cumin
2 teaspoons ground sumac
1 tablespoon sweet Hungarian paprika
½ teaspoon ground white pepper
1 tablespoon kosher salt
2 red bell peppers, roasted (jarred acceptable)
2 garlic cloves, 1 whole and 1 minced
¼ cup tahini
1 tablespoon pomegranate molasses
Leaves of 7 fresh parsley stems
¼ cup fresh mint leaves, plus 1 tablespoon chopped mint leaves
    for garnish
1 cup whole milk yogurt or labneh
1 tablespoon olive oil, or more as needed
1 pound ground lamb
1 leek, white and light green parts only, rinsed well and sliced
    into ¼-inch rounds
¾ cup chicken stock
One 10-ounce bag frozen peas
Grated zest and juice of 1 lemon
½ cup pomegranate arils (optional but highly recommended;
    they're often found in the freezer section when not in season)

1. In a small bowl, stir together the cumin, sumac, paprika, white pepper, and salt.

2. In a food processor, combine the red peppers, the whole garlic clove, the tahini, pomegranate molasses, parsley, and mint and puree until smooth. In a medium bowl, combine the puree, yogurt, and 2 tablespoons of the spice mixture and stir to combine. Set aside.

3. Heat the oil in a large sauté pan over medium-high heat. Sprinkle the remaining spice mixture over the lamb and add the

Pictured with
Bicolored Fusilli
(page 127)

lamb to the pan. Cook the lamb until it is well-browned and cooked through, stirring to break up any clumps.

4. Remove the lamb from the pan and set aside, leaving as much lamb fat in the pan as possible. If it's very lean lamb, you can add 1 more tablespoon oil to the sauté pan. Turn the heat to medium-low, add the leek, and sauté until soft, about 3 minutes. Add the minced garlic clove

and cook for 1 minute. Return the lamb to the pan, add the pepper-yogurt mixture and stock, and bring to a simmer. Turn the heat to low, add the peas and lemon zest and juice, and stir to combine. Taste for seasoning.

5. Toss with pasta and serve immediately, garnishing with the reserved chopped mint and the pomegranate arils.

'NDUJA SUGO LASAGNA WITH RICOTTA, MASCARPONE, MOZZARELLA, AND PECORINO

I know I'm breaking convention by including a lasagna recipe that doesn't use *besciamella* (béchamel), one of the most classic elements of a traditional lasagna. But I've already taken so many egregious liberties in this book that no purist police officer would dare write me a ticket, because their quill (and stamina) would run dry inking out a dozen. So here's a modern lasagna that weaves together so many hedonistic ingredients that it begs to be served at a bacchanal.

The 'nduja (spicy prosciutto paste) lends heat, but the mascarpone softens it. The pecorino provides some barnyard funk, which you can either play up by using lamb in your meat mixture or tone down by using just beef and pork. This is an important recipe to read all the way through prior to tackling, because there are some decisions to make ahead of time that will ensure your success.

MAKES ONE 9 BY 13-INCH LASAGNA | PREPARATION TIME: 2 TO 3 HOURS (BAKING TIME INACTIVE)

MEAT SAUCE

¼ cup olive oil
1 onion, finely chopped
2 pounds ground beef, or a combination of beef, lamb, and/or pork
1 tablespoon kosher salt
1 teaspoon freshly ground black pepper
5 ounces 'nduja
4 garlic cloves, minced
½ cup dry sherry
8 fresh or dried bay leaves
2 teaspoons chopped fresh thyme
One 28-ounce can crushed fire-roasted San Marzano tomatoes
   (or similar)
½ cup chicken stock

CHEESE MIXTURE

12 ounces whole milk ricotta cheese, drained in cheesecloth
   for 15 minutes
8 ounces mascarpone cheese
4 ounces Pecorino Romano cheese, grated (about ¼ cup)
4 ounces low-moisture (not water-packed) whole milk mozzarella,
   grated

2 medium eggs
1 teaspoon kosher salt
½ teaspoon freshly ground black pepper
½ teaspoon freshly grated nutmeg

1 batch Lasagne Sheets (page 87), in the color and pattern of your choice, keeping in mind that only the top 4 sheets will show (see Note)
16 ounces pre-sliced mozzarella cheese
Kosher salt (if pre-boiling)
1 tablespoon olive oil

1. To make the meat sauce, heat the oil in a large, heavy-bottomed pot over medium heat. Add the onion and sauté for 2 minutes. Increase the heat to medium-high and add the ground meat, salt, and pepper. Brown thoroughly, stirring with a wooden spoon to break up clumps. Drain off all but 2 tablespoons of the fat. Add the 'nduja and garlic and cook for 1 minute. Add the sherry, bay leaves, and thyme and cook until the sherry is reduced, about 2 minutes. Add the tomatoes, swish the stock around in the tomato can to get every last bit of tomatoes, and pour in the stock-tomato mixture. Bring to a boil, then lower the heat and simmer for at least 30 minutes, or until you have completed the other elements of the lasagna and are ready to assemble. Just before you assemble the lasagna, remove from the heat and discard the bay leaves.

2. To make the cheese mixture, combine all the ingredients in a large bowl. Use a rubber spatula to stir until smooth.

3. To assemble the lasagna, preheat the oven to 425°F. Cover the bottom of a 9 by 13-inch baking pan with a thin, even layer of the meat sauce. Place four lasagne sheets crosswise on top of the sauce. Use an offset spatula to spread a thin layer of the cheese mixture evenly on each lasagne sheet, then spoon another thin layer of meat sauce over the cheese.

4. Lay a fresh layer of lasagne sheets on top and repeat with meat sauce, cheese mixture, and lasagne sheets, ending with meat sauce and taking care to keep the filling below the top of the lasagna pan; you want to be able to protect the top lasagne sheet from cracking or burning.

5. Lay the sliced mozzarella evenly on the top layer of sauce.

6. If you've made patterned lasagne sheets for the top of the lasagna, set them aside. Cover the lasagna with aluminum foil and bake for 30 minutes, turning the pan around once halfway through. Meanwhile, very carefully boil the 4 patterned sheets in salted water for 15 seconds and lay them flat on a drying rack to cool. Remove the lasagna from the oven and place the four boiled sheets on top. Brush each sheet with a thin, even layer of oil, cover with foil, and bake for 10 minutes. Uncover and bake for 5 to 10 minutes more, or just long enough to lightly brown the top.

7. If you haven't made patterned lasagne sheets, lay the four remaining lasagne

sheets on top of the sliced mozzarella layer. Cover the lasagna with aluminum foil and bake for 40 minutes, turning the pan around once halfway through. Uncover the lasagna and bake for 5 to 10 minutes more, or just long enough to lightly brown the top.

8. Remove the lasagna from the oven and allow it to rest for 15 minutes at room temperature. Use a sharp knife to cut the lasagna into pieces, and a spatula to transport the pieces to plates to serve.

NOTE: *Pre-boiling lasagne sheets is optional. The benefit is that the pasta will absorb less moisture from the sauce, making for a saucier lasagna, but on the other hand the lasagne sheets won't stay as firm. It's a matter of textural preference. To pre-cook them, boil the sheets one at a time in salted water for 15 seconds and lay them flat on a drying rack to cool, then layer them into lasagna.*

FILLINGS

I've had some filling revelations over the years, and that's no easy feat. I mean, who has epiphanies over unsightly blobs meant to be tucked between the sheets, right? My favorite filling epiphany (stuffiphany?) has to be the moment I realized how much easier it is to make it and plop the whole blob of goop inside a zip-top bag or disposable piping bag rather than fussing with an impossible-to-clean piping bag or trying to wrangle fillings into pasta with spoons between my clumsy thumbs. Putting a filling directly into a zip-top bag or disposable piping bag solves two problems. First, storage in the fridge is easy, and second,

when it's time to fill pasta, you need only to snip the tip off a bottom corner and you're ready to pipe precise amounts of filling into the awaiting sheets.

Except for the Classic Ricotta Filling on page 255, none of these recipes is what you might consider traditional. Besides the pepperoni in the pepperoni pizza filling, there's not a speck of meat in sight. If you're really hankering for that old-school tender meat vibe, you can make the Pork Shoulder Braised in Milk and Rosé with Figs on page 242 for dinner one night, then use the leftover meaty sauce as a pasta filling the next day.

As a parent of one child, I don't have this problem, but I'm told that parents of several kids cannot choose their favorite, because they love them all equally. The same logic applies to the filling recipes that follow; I adore them all the same, and for different occasions to suit different moods. But if one were going to grow up to, say, win the Kentucky Derby of pasta fillings,

my money would be on the Pepperoni Pizza Filling on page 260, because it's an overachieving superstar I should probably rename Seabiscuit.

NOTE: *When you account for stuffing a standard batch of dough with filling, you'll wind up with more than four servings because of the total volume of pasta plus filling.*

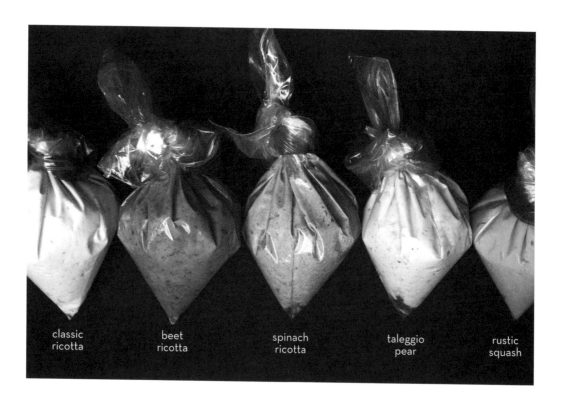

classic ricotta   beet ricotta   spinach ricotta   taleggio pear   rustic squash

CLASSIC RICOTTA FILLING

This filling is a generous dollop of *la vita bella*. You can spruce it up with additions like spinach, beets, or nettles or go in a completely different direction and cradle whole egg yolks inside a nest of filling to make dinner plate–size ravioloni (see page 263).

MAKES PLENTY OF FILLING FOR 1 BATCH OF DOUGH (SEE NOTE ON PAGE 254)
PREPARATION TIME: 5 MINUTES PLUS 15 MINUTES DRAINING TIME

1 egg yolk
One 15-ounce tub whole milk ricotta cheese, drained in cheesecloth
    for 15 minutes
1 cup finely grated Parmigiano-Reggiano cheese
½ teaspoon kosher salt
¼ teaspoon freshly ground black pepper
½ teaspoon freshly grated nutmeg
1 teaspoon sugar

1. Combine all the ingredients in a medium bowl and stir until the mixture is well combined and resembles the texture of soft-serve ice cream. Do not overmix or the filling will become too thin. I like to mix this by hand rather than in a stand mixer or food processor because it's easy to both see and feel when the ingredients come together without going too far.

2. Using a rubber spatula, scrape the filling into a gallon-size zip-top bag or disposable piping bag. Seal the bag and refrigerate for at least 30 minutes, or until needed. The filling keeps for 3 days.

VARIATIONS

SPINACH RICOTTA FILLING

3 ounces baby spinach leaves, washed (2 large handfuls)

In a blender (or using an immersion blender), puree the spinach leaves with the egg yolk and 1/4 cup of the ricotta until smooth. Combine this puree with the rest of the ingredients and proceed as directed on page 255.

BEET RICOTTA FILLING

1 medium red beet

Wrap the beet in a moist paper towel and microwave on high for 5 minutes. It will not be completely soft; don't be alarmed. When it's cool enough to handle, peel the beet and grate it on the medium holes of a box grater into a medium bowl. Add the rest of the ingredients and proceed as as directed on page 255.

Spinach Ricotta Filling

Rustic Squash Filling

TALEGGIO PEAR FILLING

I want this filling to sing at my funeral. It's the Lady Gaga of pasta fillings—smooth and white but filled with soul. It works best for smaller-size filled pasta, such as agnolotti, as it is so lush that it deserves to be relished one dainty bite at a time. You could technically use any cheese with a triple-crème-like texture, but Taleggio plays so nicely with sage, balsamic, and pears that it was a no-brainer to specify it.

MAKES PLENTY OF FILLING FOR 1 BATCH OF DOUGH (SEE NOTE ON PAGE 254)
PREPARATION TIME: 20 MINUTES

One 1-ounce wedge of Taleggio cheese, rind removed, cut into 1-inch chunks
1 medium-sweet pear, such as Anjou or Bartlett, peeled, seeded, and cut into 1-inch chunks
1 teaspoon balsamic vinegar (use the best quality you can find)
1 teaspoon olive oil
7 large fresh sage leaves
1/3 cup heavy cream
1/4 cup freshly grated Parmigiano-Reggiano cheese
1/4 teaspoon kosher salt
1/4 teaspoon freshly ground black pepper
1 medium russet potato, baked, peeled, and riced or mashed smooth (do not food process—too gloppy)

1. Combine the Taleggio, pear, and vinegar in a blender or food processor.

2. Heat the oil in a small saucepan over medium heat. Add the sage leaves and fry for 1 minute per side, until they just start to brown at the edges and the aroma of sage fills the air. Stir in the cream and remove from the heat when it comes just to a simmer.

3. Pour the cream and sage into the blender and add the Parmigiano, salt, and pepper. Blend to a smooth puree, scraping down the bowl as necessary.

4. Put the potato in a medium bowl. Using a silicone spatula, fold the Taleggio puree into the potato just until it is well combined. Don't overmix or the filling will become runny.

5. Scrape the filling into a gallon-size zip-top bag or disposable piping bag and refrigerate for at least 1 hour or up to 24 hours.

RUSTIC SQUASH FILLING

I recommend using a medium-sweet winter squash such as butternut or delicata for this recipe. Butternut will be much easier to peel, but delicata does have an undeniably lovely flavor that makes it worth it to either peel or scoop out the flesh.

MAKES PLENTY OF FILLING FOR 1 BATCH OF DOUGH (SEE NOTE ON PAGE 254)
PREPARATION TIME: 25 MINUTES

3 cups 1-inch chunks of peeled, seeded, chopped winter squash,
    such as butternut or delicata
½ cup whole milk ricotta cheese, drained in cheesecloth
    for 15 minutes
1 egg yolk
1 tablespoon sugar
1 teaspoon kosher salt
½ teaspoon freshly ground black pepper
½ teaspoon freshly grated nutmeg

1. Place the squash in a medium heatproof bowl and cover tightly with plastic wrap. Microwave on high for 4 minutes.

2. Put the steamed squash in a food processor and let cool for 5 minutes. Add the remaining ingredients and process until smooth. You may have to scrape down the sides of the processor a few times to incorporate all the ingredients.

3. Using a rubber spatula, scrape the filling into a gallon-size zip-top bag or disposable piping bag. Seal the bag and refrigerate for at least 30 minutes, or until needed. The filling keeps for 3 days.

BURRATA FILLING

If you've spent hours making a stunning pattern meant for the giant ravioloni on page 159, you might not want to spend additional hours cobbling together a filling too. At the same time, you don't want all that labor to go unnoticed because your filling is ho-hum. Enter the burrata filling: a show-stopping hack.

Burrata is a genius ravioloni filling because it's easy for *you* but tastes like the height of decadence. The oozy inside of the taut ball of mozzarella is filled with velvety *stracciatella* that gushes from the rav when you slice into it. It's low-fuss wow factor at its very best.

Plan for one 4-ounce ball of burrata inside one raviolone per person—trust me, it's so rich that it's enough. Reach to the back of the cheese refrigerator and select a tub of burrata (usually there are two balls per tub) with as distant an expiration date as you can find. It has a short shelf life, and you wouldn't want to diminish all your hard work by serving funky cheese.

MAKES 4 SINGLE-SERVING RAVIOLONI | PREPARATION TIME: 2 MINUTES!

Four 4-ounce balls burrata (usually two 8-ounce tubs)
Flour
Kosher salt

1. Just before placing the burrata on the bottom pasta sheet, wipe it gently with a paper towel to try to absorb any moisture that may cause the pasta to tear. Place a small pinch of flour on the bottom pasta sheet where the burrata will rest and rub it around with your index finger so it covers the base everywhere the burrata touches. One end of the burrata will be more open. Make sure the other, more solid end is resting on the bottom sheet, or you risk the curds oozing out.

2. Before covering the burrata with the top pasta sheet, dust it gently with flour to absorb additional moisture. See the sealing instructions on page 167. Hold the filled pasta in the refrigerator, uncovered, for no more than 8 hours before boiling.

3. Be sure to boil the sealed ravioloni no more than four at a time in a large salted stockpot. Ravioloni filled with burrata boiled for 3 minutes will yield a filling that is warmed through but still firm. If you want the filling even more melt-in-your-mouth, you can go up to 4 minutes.

PEPPERONI PIZZA FILLING

Pepperoni is a point of contention for most Italians. You see, *peperoni*—with just one "p" in the middle—are large peppers in Italian, so a peperoni pizza is one with peppers on it. What Americans think of as pepperoni is really salami, and one that was created on United States soil, not Italian, since you're unlikely to find that bastardized flavor combination in the motherland. When Italians first see pepperoni on pizzeria menus in the United States, they are no doubt thinking, "Not only can these *stronzi* not make pizza; they also can't spell worth a damn." I guess Americans have the last laugh when the pizza comes out full of meat, not peppers, but in the end, everyone is happy because pepperoni tastes so transcendental that it could unite the world.

You may think it sounds strange to stuff pasta sheets with pepperoni pizza ingredients, but perfect flavor combinations should be experienced in myriad ways, no? I mean, I wouldn't kick a pepperoni pizza taco out of bed.

This filling is not as smooth and homogenous as some of the others, which adds to its charm and makes it better for larger filled pasta, such as ravioloni (see page 159). Because of the texture, instead of storing it in a zip-top bag like the other fillings, I recommend pre-batching it into individual discs. This saves time down the line when you've just made an elaborate pasta pattern and don't want to mess with rolling gooey filling between your floury pasta hands. MAKES ENOUGH FILLING FOR 8 RAVIOLONI; ONE PERSON CAN EAT 1 AS AN APPETIZER, 2 AS A MAIN COURSE | PREPARATION TIME: 15 MINUTES

8 ounces low-moisture (not water-packed) whole milk mozzarella
   cheese, roughly chopped
3 ounces pepperoni slices (or other sliced salami of your choice, such
   as sopressata)
¼ cup canned tomato sauce
16 fresh basil leaves
Flour, for forming balls of filling

1. Combine the mozzarella, pepperoni, tomato sauce, and basil in a food processor and pulse until the mixture is uniform but still textured, with no large chunks. Do not overmix this filling or it will become unpleasantly grainy.

2. Remove the filling en masse to a floured work surface and divide it into eight portions. Roll each portion together with floured hands as if you were making meatballs. Flatten the balls into discs about 1 inch thick. Store on a parchment-

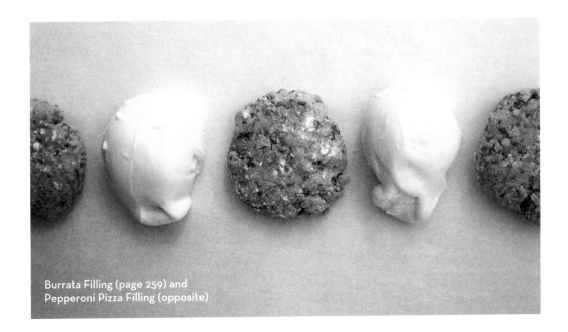

Burrata Filling (page 259) and
Pepperoni Pizza Filling (opposite)

lined, floured sheet pan, covered, if using within 3 hours; otherwise cover the pan and refrigerate for up to 24 hours. Following the directions on page 167, fill and seal the ravioloni.

3. Be sure to boil the sealed ravioloni no more than four at a time in a large stockpot. Boil ravioloni made with this filling for 4 minutes, so that the mozzarella has enough time in the hot water to melt. The ooziness cannot be beat. Since there's plenty going on both aesthetically and inside the ravioloni, there's no need for a complicated sauce. I recommend any of the browned butters starting on page 202.

EGG YOLK RAVIOLONI

This is a filling and boiling technique for ravioloni—giant ravioli—of any pattern, such as emoji (see page 159). It combines several things: your chosen pasta pattern, a delicious ricotta filling, and egg yolks. The glorious guts of this pasta gush onto the dinner plate in the form of soft, golden yolk, and while you could boil the pasta longer to cook the egg, it would not only overcook the pasta, it would also ruin the magic of this dish. In other words, make this for soft-cooked egg lovers and they'll be in heaven. I recommend serving no more than one raviolone per person as an extravagant course in a larger meal, as they are the savory world's indulgent equivalent to chocolate mousse.

You can dress this pasta with any of the browned butters that start on page 202, or even plain melted butter will do, as the sauce is already on the inside of these ethereal creatures.

It's very important that you have all of the ingredients and tools prepared and ready for use, as this filling is a bit of a race against the clock. At first, make one raviolone at a time. As you become more agile at the process, you can make two or three at a time, but remember, you don't want your pasta sheets to dry out while you're fussing with filling them.   MAKES 6 RAVIOLONI, TO SERVE 6

SPECIAL EQUIPMENT
A pastry brush
A larger diameter (4 inches or thereabouts) round cookie cutter is helpful
   but not necessary (you'll use the blunt end, not the cutting edge)
Whichever rolling cutter you wish to use to cut the edges of the ravioloni
3 small bowls: 1 for the egg white you need, 1 for shells, and 1 for the egg
   whites you don't need

Pasta sheets from 1 batch of dough, rolled to the second-thinnest setting
   on a pasta machine (if you're using emoji patterns, prepare just 1 or 2 at
   a time so they don't dry out)
1 batch ricotta (see page 255), spinach ricotta (see page 256), or beet
   ricotta (see page 256) filling
Flour
6 eggs, chilled (do not crack the eggs until the moment called for, and you
   may need a few extra in case of breakage)
1 egg white
Six ⅛-inch slices of butter taken from the square end of a standard stick
   (keep in the fridge until needed)
Semolina
Kosher salt

1. Work with pasta sheets that are pre-cut into 5- to 6-inch squares. Keep all the pasta sheets not currently in use covered with a kitchen towel so that they don't dry out.

2. Cut a ½-inch piece off the corner of the zip-top bag containing the filling. Use your index finger to lightly flour the middle of a base pasta sheet.

3. Pipe a nest of ricotta filling in a 3-inch-diameter circle about 1 inch high. Leave the center of the circle free of filling; this is where you will place your egg yolk.

4. Separate the eggs, reserving all but one of the whites for later use. Place a yolk in the middle of the ricotta nest very gently, so as not to break it. If you break a yolk, scoop the whole mess off the base

pasta sheet and try again, as broken yolks won't cook properly.

5. Gently top the egg yolk with a slice of the butter, rounding it to conform to the yolk if it's malleable enough. Use a pastry brush to brush the base sheet with the egg white around the filling nest so that the top sheet will adhere to it. Uncover a top sheet and align it over the base sheet, pattern side up. Very gently set the top sheet over the base and egg nest, taking care to push air bubbles to the edges and avoid wrinkling the top sheet.

6. The blunt side (*not the sharp side*) of a round cookie cutter will work very well here to smooth all the bubbles and flatten the top sheet to the base sheet. Just roll the upside-down cutter in a gentle, circular motion around the egg nest until the pasta is smooth and there is a nice, defined line between the flat part of the raviolone and the nest.

7. Because there is so much flat surface area stuck together with egg white, you do not technically have to cut these ravioloni to crimp them, but you may if you wish. You can keep them as squares, or even turn your cookie cutter over and cut them into circles. Bear in mind that the more pasta you leave on the ravioloni, the more you'll get to eat later. I prefer 4¼-inch flute-edged squares, but you've come this far, so put your own spin on it if you wish.

8. Repeat steps 3 to 7 using the remaining 5 eggs and butter slices.

9. Store the ravioloni uncovered on parchment-lined, semolina-dusted sheet pans. They can be kept at room

temperature for up to 2 hours or uncovered in the refrigerator for up to 6 hours.

10. Use as large a stockpot as you can for these and boil 2 or 3 at a time in salted water for 4 minutes. Drain, dress, and serve immediately.

ACKNOWLEDGMENTS

One person may write a book, but it takes a village to raise it, bail it out of teenage jams, get it off to college, and finally foist it upon the world in one piece. Many thanks to the village of *Pasta, Pretty Please*. Thank you to everyone at the William Morrow imprint of HarperCollins, starting with my patient, tireless, genius (like, I think she wrote the Mensa test) editor, Cassie Jones. I have no idea how I got lucky enough for her to not only reach out to me, but also to continue to want to work with me, even after discovering my unique brand of insanity. And thank you to the rest of the team: Kara Zauberman, Liate Stehlik, Lynn Grady, Tavia Kowalchuk, Maria Silva, Rachel Meyers, Renata De Oliveira, and Anna Brower.

Next up, Brittany Wright, whose images brought this book to life, and whose advice sometimes keeps me alive. Ashley Collom, for being the pit bull to my golden retriever. Thank you to those who helped with the nuts and bolts of this book, both in and out of the kitchen: Kristi Welsh, Laurie Boucher, Rita Miller, Jonas Nicholson, and Margaret Arakawa.

Lastly, thank you to all the powerful women in my life, who acted as soundboards and offered wisdom, humor, inspiration, and encouragement. I'm proud that so many of us are finally taking a seat at the table.

PUBLISHED WORKS I'D LIKE TO THANK

The Oxford English Dictionary by Oxford Dictionaries (Oxford University Press, various editions)

> For being my bedtime reading, my stress ball, my moral compass, and my favorite novel-that-is-not-a-novel from the time I was big enough to hoist it into my lap until now.

The Love Song of J. Alfred Prufrock by T. S. Eliot (*Poetry: A Magazine of Verse*, 1915)

> This poem is the reason I dared to write. Because of it, I strive to live boldly and without regret. It gives me something new and vast every time I read it. T. S. Eliot is my hall pass.

The Moosewood Cookbook by Mollie Katzen (Ten Speed Press, 1977)

> For encouraging experimentation and instilling a profound love of vegetables.

The Vegetarian Epicure, Book Two by Anna Thomas (Knopf, 1978)

> For fettuccine Alfredo, however cheesy it may be, and for giving me wanderlust through food.

Romantic Italian Cooking by Mary Cadogan (HP Trade, 1986)

> For keeping a child's hands occupied, and getting a mother and daughter through divorce.

Giuliano Bugialli's Classic Techniques of Italian Cooking by Giuliano Bugialli (Simon & Schuster, 1982)

> For giving me structure and respect for tradition before I was able to experience it for myself.

The Mozza Cookbook by Nancy Silverton with Matt Molina and Carolynn Carreño (Knopf, 2011)

> For showing me there was something to come home to.

UNIVERSAL CONVERSION CHART

OVEN TEMPERATURE EQUIVALENTS

250°F = 120°C

275°F = 135°C

300°F = 150°C

325°F = 160°C

350°F = 180°C

375°F = 190°C

400°F = 200°C

425°F = 220°C

450°F = 230°C

475°F = 240°C

500°F = 260°C

MEASUREMENT EQUIVALENTS

Measurements should always be level unless directed otherwise.

⅛ teaspoon = 0.5 mL

¼ teaspoon = 1 mL

½ teaspoon = 2 mL

1 teaspoon = 5 mL

1 tablespoon = 3 teaspoons = ½ fluid ounce = 15 mL

2 tablespoons = ⅛ cup = 1 fluid ounce = 30 mL

4 tablespoons = ¼ cup = 2 fluid ounces = 60 mL

5⅓ tablespoons = ⅓ cup = 3 fluid ounces = 80 mL

8 tablespoons = ½ cup = 4 fluid ounces = 120 mL

10⅔ tablespoons = ⅔ cup = 5 fluid ounces = 160 mL

12 tablespoons = ¾ cup = 6 fluid ounces = 180 mL

16 tablespoons = 1 cup = 8 fluid ounces = 240 mL

INDEX

Note: Page references in *italics* indicate photographs.